LOWER THAN VERM

Author (left) with editor Rowson, 1983 *(photograph copyright P. K. Guzley)*

Kevin Killane was born in Jannali, New South Wales, in 1938. After taking his Ph.D. in comparative sociology at the London School of Economics, he held positions at a number of Universities, including Chicago and the University of East Anglia. Apart from writing, researching and teaching, Dr Killane spends most of his time travelling, and spent a considerable time during the 1970s in Vietnam, but does return home occasionally, to a small house in Holland Park which he owns with his ex-wife, the feminist critic Helen Killane.

Dr Killane's previous books include *The Dialectics of Monetarism, Mao and Marcuse: The Gerontocracy of the New Left, The Lost Vortecist*, a biography of the poet Julian Sykes-Wolsey, and *The Bestiary: Zoos, Zoo Animals and the Weltschmertz*, a book about Man's troubled and ambiguous relationship with animals. The synthesis of his experiences in Vietnam, *The Moon and Napalm: Journeys to a Free Saigon*, was hailed by *Village Voice* as 'a Counter Culture classic' when it appeared in 1976.

Martin Rowson was born in London in 1959, and has been a full-time free-lance cartoonist since leaving University in 1982. Apart from regular appearances in a wide variety of magazines, and occasional work for the Royal Shakespeare Company, a series of cartoons drawn for *New Statesman* formed the basis of *Scenes from the Lives of the Great Socialists*, his first book written with Kevin Killane.

BIBLIOGRAPHY OF KEVIN KILLANE

A Norfolk Agricultural Community and Subsistence Farming in the Babylonian Empire, Cromer Hand Press, 1960

Piety and Peyote: The Catholic Conquest of Central America, Notre Dame, 1966

The Dialectics of Monetarism, Chicago, 1966

Mao and Marcuse: The Gerontocracy of the New Left, Seven Seas, 1968

The Language of Transport: Cultural and Structural Meanings of the Ho Chi Minh Trail, Simon and Schuster, 1970

The Moon and Napalm: Journeys to a Free Saigon, Random House, 1976

The Lost Vortecist: A Biography of Julian Sykes-Wolsey, OUP, 1978

Selections from the Poetry and Prose of Isaac Guillespie, Faber, 1981

From Mensch to Messiah: An Appreciation of Isaac Guillespie, Poetry Society, 1981

The Bestiary: Zoos, Zoo Animals and the Weltschmertz, Pathfinder, 1982

WITH MARTIN ROWSON

Scenes from the Lives of the Great Socialists, Grapheme Publications, 1983

WITH HELEN KILLANE

Living Together After Divorce: A Practical Guide, Routledge and Kegan Paul, 1978

The Conventions of Convenience: A Sociology of Public Lavatories, Gay Sunshine Press, 1984

WITH DAVID ZEITLYN

Archaeology and Anthropology in Hollywood: From 'The Mummy's Curse' to 'Raiders of the Lost Ark', Blackwells, 1985

LOWER THAN VERMIN

An anatomy of Thatcher's Britain

Kevin Killane

edited and illustrated by
Martin Rowson

ARROW BOOKS

For Anna, without whom, in all likelihood, nothing would be possible; Dave, who's seen the
light at last, and Sam, who's yet to learn that
the following is the truth . . .

ACKNOWLEDGEMENTS

I would like to thank the following people for
their invaluable assistance in the production of
this book:

Charles Adley, Faith Brooker, Robert and Ann
Buttimore, Anna Clarke, Freebase Kevin, Pete
Illsley, Dexter Jakes, Mary-Lou Jennings, Abi-
gail Jones, Helen Killane, Michael Kuczynski,
Jon Lewin, Little Jon, Rosemary Medlam, Anna
Raine, David Ramseyer, Peter Ricketts, Dr and
Mrs K. E. K. Rowson, Roger Scruton, Graham
Shuttleworth, Ingrid Swenson, Shaun White-
side, John Wright and David Zeitlyn.

Designed by Roger Walker/Linde Hardaker

The cartoons on pages 69 and 83 first appeared in
Radical magazine and *END Journal* respectively

Arrow Books Limited
62–65 Chandos Place, London WC2N 4NW

An imprint of Century Hutchinson Ltd

London Melbourne Sydney Auckland
Johannesburg and agencies throughout
the world

First published 1986

© Kevin Killane and Martin Rowson 1986

Set in Century Schoolbook by
Rowland Phototypesetting Ltd, Bury St Edmunds

Printed and bound in Great Britain by
Butler and Tanner Ltd, Frome, Somerset

ISBN 0 09 944650 2

INTRODUCTION

BY MARTIN ROWSON

It might be thought rather peculiar to ask oneself, at the point of writing the introduction to a book one has spent many months preparing for publication, 'But what does it all *mean*?' with reference to that book, but looking through *Lower Than Vermin* one last time before it goes to the presses, I can't help wondering.

After all, what's this book meant to be? I'm sure readers familiar with the previous works of Kevin Killane, the noted Australian critic and academic, will be as puzzled as I continue to be when they turn the page and read on. Is this Killane's contribution to the literature of travel? For at its simplest level it is merely a series of reflections upon a number of topics during what I can only describe as a whistle-stop, round-the-world trip undertaken by Killane between May and October 1985. But then, looking further, it suddenly seems nothing of the sort, and turns into political analysis of the state of Britain under Mrs Thatcher. But if it's that, why did Killane find it necessary to undertake what I've roughly calculated as a journey of 50,000 miles to achieve what other people do sitting in newspaper offices every day of the year? And then there's all this stuff about animals. Is Killane merely indulging that passion that readers of *The Bestiary: Zoos, Zoo Animals and the Weltschmertz* will recognize, or is he trying to say something deeper? And, if so, what?

In order to clarify things a little, I should perhaps outline how this book came into existence. Firstly, I should explain that Killane did not actually write it: its first draft exists on about ten or twelve cassette tapes, dictated on an extended holiday taken after the termination of his contract at the University of The West Indies. These came into my possession *via* Dexter Jakes, a former colleague of Killane's from the University of Chicago, to whom Killane had sent them from his various points of repose. And yet the tapes are not letters to Jakes, and only with the sixth or seventh package did he receive the instruction to get me to edit and illustrate them and turn them into some kind of book. As Killane put it in his scrawled note: 'Get Rowson onto this, he owes me for SLUGS' (which I take as a reference to our first collaboration, *Scenes from the Lives of the Great Socialists*).

So what was his motive in making the tapes? It could just be that Killane had a bee in his bonnet about Thatcherism, and chose this medium of expiation. And yet that seems far too simple, if I know anything about Killane, and I'm certain there must be something deeper about the whole business, although I'm presently at a loss to say exactly what it is.

Some light – though not much – is thrown by a comment of Helen Killane's, the feminist critic and the Doctor's ex-wife: 'Kevin's problem is he's always running away, then thinking up a reason why while he's running.' Are the circumstances behind *Lower Than Vermin* the result of a reaction to Thatcherism every bit as telling as what he actually says in the book: to wit, flight?

Still, I should really leave exegeses on motive and content to the reader – for me to speak here of Thatcherism would be to steal the Doctor's thunder.

And thunder he certainly does. Indeed, some people may see this book as little more than a hopelessly biased and unfair rant, and they might have a point. After all, in attacking Thatcherism Killane offers no alternative; similarly, he assumes his audience shares his opinions most of the time, and doesn't bother himself too much with a statistician's analysis of The Thatcher Government. Then again, that's been done often enough in the past, and he has (I assume) other intentions which, again, I leave to the reader to judge.

A few words, then, on my part in all of this. My contribution has been to transcribe the tapes (which has not always been easy: I regret to say that Killane's apparent silence between July and October is not, in fact, because of a sudden period of taciturnity affecting him, but because the package from Ulan Bator was so full of sand that the tape was rendered inaudible, and so Killane's opinions on Thatcher's foreign policy have been lost to the winds of the city of tents and magic); to edit them, which has involved little more than attempts on my part to capture Killane's written prose style, which differs from his aural style only in the use of perceived punctuation (for an example of real written Killane, see the section 'A Mad World, My Masters'); and then to illustrate the text. In this last, I have endeavoured to adhere to the spirit of the words, and can only hope Killane is happy with the result. I was working on a book about otters before Killane re-entered my life after almost two years, and I have not, in fact, either met or spoken to him since 1983, so if my contribution isn't up to his scratch, I think I can get away with saying that this isn't really my fault.

In conclusion, I should point out that this book is not, of course, the last word on Thatcherism. It is, rather, one man's view of Thatcher's Britain received and communicated during a brief period in the summer and autumn of last year. Inevitably, as this is not a newspaper, many of the *dramatis personae* are no longer strutting around on the stage, and the political memory being short, the victims and quitters portrayed might seem now to be like beings from a by-gone age. And yet, if you cast your mind back to that strange time, yesterday or a thousand years ago, when Michael Heseltine was still Defence Secretary, Leon Brittan was at the Home Office, Patrick Jenkin still struggled at the Department of the Environment or, indeed (and who knows what might happen between the time of writing and publication of this?), when Mrs Thatcher occupied No. 10, you'll see what follows as a powerful indictment, and an interesting personal judgement, on Thatcherism's mid-life crisis by a remarkable, if sometimes rather peculiar, intellect.

LONDON, JANUARY 1986

DARK REMEMBRANCE OF FOREST FRIENDS

'No attempt at ethical or social seduction can
eradicate from my heart a deep, burning hatred for
the Tory Party . . . So far as I am concerned, they are
lower than vermin'   ANEURIN BEVAN

The human mind, as many intelligent people have had cause to observe in the past, is a curious thing. In view of this I can only wonder at why the words quoted above – which the more po-faced Establishment commentators insist lost Labour the 1951 General Election – should suddenly have crossed my mind. Nor do I necessarily wish to enter into a game of reversed grandmother's whispers to find out the source of this train of thought. Nor, indeed, do I know why remembrances of Bevan have been supplanted by disagreeable memories of a day spent at the London Zoo almost two years ago.

It was either just before or just after the 1983 British election that, accompanied by the cartoonist Martin Rowson, I visited the Zoo, of which I have been a scientific fellow since 1981[1]. It was shortly after the enforced closure of my own collection in Camden, and I suggested to Rowson, who was badgering me for a meal to celebrate our clinching the deal for our first collaboration[2], that we dine at my club, as I was hankering, for various now forgotten reasons, for the company of animals in the only club in London with its own menagerie.

And so it was, after a heavy lunch (they then did the best crab soup in town) during which Rowson drank a great deal of the agreeable house wine (which, incidentally, has a zebra on the label), that we went for a stroll round the gardens.

Now, I know as well as the next man that zoos are suffering a bad press at the moment, and that the weasel words of the Militant Animalist Lobby call for their closure, the opening of the cages and the liberation of the creatures to roam and prowl the city streets, grazing in suburban gardens and devouring all in their path, but, unreconstructed as I am, I like zoos. To those sentimentalists who insist that the animals are unhappy, I say: how do you *know*? How can you be sure that they weren't far unhappier in the wild, constantly under threat of being eaten, hunted, drowned, struck by lightning, trapped and dying young and miserable? And I would go further in this argument: if I'm obliged to accept that all the animals in the Zoo are morose and neurotic, then I will argue that just as Metropolitan Man is an unnatural creature plagued by a thousand and one neuroses so he needs his equally neurotic Metropolitan Familiars. But, worse still in the eyes of the Gugnuncs of the anti-zoo brigade, principally I find a lot of the animals *very funny*.

---

[1] Elected on the strength of *The Bestiary: Zoos, Zoo Animals and the Weltschmertz*.
[2] *Scenes from the Lives of the Great Socialists*, Grapheme Publications, 1983.

That said, I should add that I also hold a great respect for these beasts, and for none more than for the orang-utan. I can never visit the Zoo without paying a call on the Great Apes Breeding House, which at that time was housing the animal to whom I am utterly beholden, an orang-utan of mighty proportions who lived there with his mate. (I say *lived* because, on my last visit, I was horrified to see my friends' place taken by a troop of those most tedious of anthropomorphs, chimpanzees, whose species extinction would be a loss to no one except a few ghoulish behavioural psychologists on the West Coast of the United States.) Anyway, on that occasion the orang-utans were still in residence and happily going about their daily business: she daintily picking up pieces of orange peel, grooming herself and generally tidying the place up, while he, typical of his sex, sat all the day long doing absolutely nothing, with not a care in the world and a quite obvious contempt for those other apes who came to gawp. Not for him the hurly-burly of city life, the stresses of civilization, the pitfalls and bugbears of obligations and responsibilities in the Modern World. Not for him (and I was mindful of then current events) agonizings over the money supply, mawkish thoughts of small businessmen, or sleepless nights behind the bars fretting over the prospects for enterprise as he nibbled specks of salt picked nimbly from his wife's pelt. Instead he just sat, chewing the occasional orange, sticking straws in his ears, climbing into and out of old potato sacks and, now and again, hurling an ancient bald tyre against the walls of his cage, and quite clearly determined to betray his injunction to breed. But why should that be? Was it that whatever potent juices had once lurked within his saffron loins had long since ceased to flow? Or, alternatively, bestial though he was, had he sworn himself to a life of celibacy to some unknown god of the Sumatran rain forest? No, it could be neither of those, for, as he fixed you with a loathing glower in his beady little eyes and tipped some more stinky old rubbish over his head, it became plain what he was telling you, as plain as if he hissed it contemptuously through the bars: 'If you think we're going to have a fuck with all you bastards watching, you've got another think coming.'

But perhaps it goes further than this. Realizing his status as Metropolitan Familiar, perhaps the ape embarked upon a personal regime of voluntary celibacy, the better to match the society in which he finds himself captive. Which might explain something infinitely disturbing I noticed as I stood gazing lovingly at my old friend (I'd left Rowson in maudlin communion with the wombats some time before). It's the memory of this sudden awareness that's sent me off on this freefall association of memory, *via* Bevan, to the Zoo: *The orang-utan looked exactly like William Whitelaw.*

FURTHER REFLECTIONS ON DUMB CHUMS

Of course, it is a preposterous idea that Viscount Whitelaw, slumped and vegetating in the House of Lords and now and again wobbling to his feet to flap his dewlaps in half-hearted and wary support of some more highly peculiar government legislation, could really be an orang-utan, either shaved and stuffed into a suit or else the victim of some latter-day Dr Moreau. Or is it? Isn't it just possible that we've all been duped by some monstrous, barely conceivable conspiracy by the Animal Liberation Front to wreak a terrible revenge on humankind's speciocentric wickedness, and that Britain is actually ruled not by the heirs to Coke and Hampden but by a Government of Dumb Chums, cack-handedly transformed into vague simulacrums of human beings? There is

a kind of insane logic to it: dump on the humes really viciously, deprive them of their jobs, their civil liberties, their city fastnesses, their Welfare State and, as the final kamikaze gesture of organic rage, blow the buggers to bits!

Did Bevan know more than we ever dared imagine? Is it just chance that Margaret Thatcher bears a marked physical resemblance to a hyena, despite the fact that she seldom laughs? That Norman Tebbit looks exactly like a Tyrannosaurus Rex (I wouldn't put time travel past these scheming fiends)? We can go further. Has Geoffrey Howe never reminded you of a manatee or seacow? Nigel Lawson of an elephant seal? Leon Brittan of a poisonous toad? Michael Heseltine of an obscene combination of wolverine and sink plunger? And then, outside the Cabinet, there is Francis Pym looking for all the world like a particularly revolting species of deep sea fish, and Cecil Parkinson, if we admit the vegetable constituency into the scheme of things, looking like a mushroom. Chuck in a few liver flukes and bacterial cultures behind the Treasury benches and there you have it . . .

But perhaps it isn't really as easy as all that. Speculating on this in the VIP lounge of Tongan Royal Airways, awaiting my connection to Nuku'alofa, I am given pause. For I share the room with a vast Tongan prince reading comic books and, as I saw with fear and horror as I entered the room, a former pupil of mine from UEA. Unfortunately, the latter saw me before I could back away, and has since settled down to tell me how he's risen from Social Secretary of the Students' Union to the position of economic adviser in the Prime Minister's Office. And it seems that he, too, has given himself up to travel, and after six weeks on manoeuvres with the Contras in Honduras, he's now on his way from an audience with Mrs Jeanne Kirkpatrick to an International 'Youth for Freedom' Exposition in the Pacific. Thus I am subjected to several hours of incessant jabbering about 'Wealth Creators', 'The Enterprise Culture', 'Venture Capitalism' and other modish gibberish which he somehow considers of interest to an itinerant man of letters like myself.

And it occurs to me that the theriomorphic analysis will not, after all, do. For, despite a certain historical tradition in the Tory Party – one could cite the Duke of Wellington's small and vestigial tail, the fact that Balfour was never seen naked (what was he hiding? fur? horny scales?) – one cannot account current phenomena to an evolutionary throwback or dark lycanthropy. However diverting it may be to imagine Thatcher reverting to type at the full moon and snuffling her snout into the spilled guts of a gnu on the floor of the Cabinet room, or Geoffrey Howe basking for plankton in the Serpentine, the fact remains that our four-footed, feathery and flippered friends are very Platos and Adonises compared to these grubby creatures.

And animals, at least, are blessed by the lack of articulate speech, unlike this smooth young maniac, with his chin now thrust into my shoulder just like the Duchess in *Alice in Wonderland* and his wild words about great adventures, bliss to be alive, the glorious new dawn, jobs to be done, and light at the end of the tunnel. All of which suggests, as I drag my thoughts reluctantly from jungle and tundra to try to make sense of what he's saying to me, that here we have a genuine Thatcherite, the real McCoy, fantasy made some kind of flesh. But what, then, is Thatcherism? I suspect, for all his fine words, he would be unable to tell me; nor, for that matter, could Thatcher herself. For what can one say of a philosophy – philosophy? – that seeks to eradicate generations of political and social evolution and replace it with a bit of dubious homespun wisdom and grocer's shop nostalgia? Indeed, if I myself were forced to give a definition, the currency of conventional political analysis would seem redundant.

And yet, observing my former pupil from the corner of my eye, and half listening to his paeans about the small businessman and how he'd been involved in an attempt to have Arthur Scargill indicted for treason, a pat definition occurs: Mr Pooter meets Lord Castlereagh.

□   □   □

It's now the 22nd of May (which sounds, possibly, like the name of an Argentine cruiser) and there's still no sight of this plane.

The Tongan prince has lain down on the floor of the VIP lounge and gone to sleep, not unsurprisingly, and his snores have driven the Thatcherite munchkin off to complain to 'someone in authority here'. So much for libertarianism. But at least this gives me time to reflect.

And in so doing I return to my thoughts of yesterday.

Put simply, Thatcherism is best explained as that philosophy which seeks to create a New Jerusalem based on the high principles of the Ideal Home Exhibition, its hymns couched in the rhetoric of the tupperware party.

Whether this definition would please either my old chums on *Marxism Today* or the babbling *Sturms* of the Centre for Policy Studies I cannot say, but it seems to summarize the phenomenon well enough for our purposes here. There is, after all, a quite distinct mood abroad, one which came with Thatcherism and may even have been created by it. It is manifested by bitter tears and howls of impotent rage everywhere from the Established Church, the Professors of Oxford and the House of Lords down to most of the population living north of Brighton; and elsewhere, in the right wing Think Tanks of Belgravia, the common rooms of Oxbridge colleges and the new towns, by a wild excitement, by the celebration of a new, vibrant radicalism and the apotheosis of Bracknell.

But, beyond despair or elation, what is the state of Thatcher's Britain, seven years in, when the dream might be about to collapse but while we're still in the heart of the beast? It might prove amusing, even now, to take another look at that failed dream of England, this thing 'Thatcherism', build on those dark thoughts of the forest, and try to see where we're going with this interregnum in the continuity of Butskellism that accompanies Britain in her final decline.

In her final decline? Not a concept to appeal to the Thatcherites, but suggested both elegantly and wheezingly by the Earl of Stockton in a recent debate in the House of Lords. Unless something was done, Stockton said (without making it too clear what that something should be), Britain would sink slowly, magnificently, like a liner of old, into the chill but boiling ocean. Which, lachrymose though it is, is a rather pleasing image. The string quartet still playing agreeable tunes of old Vienna as it slips gently across the floor, women and children forming orderly queues for the non-existent lifeboats and the Captain,

crew and first class passengers stiffening the sinews, fixing their upper lips into a steadfast grimace and preparing to die with honour intact, while the poor schmucks down in steerage drown in the bilge.

No U-turns, Cap'n Thatcher? Then aim for that Iceberg, and full steam ahead!

NUKU'ALOFA, TONGA, 27 MAY 1985

The plane, despite the weird bad magic of my former pupil, finally arrived, my depression lifted, and now in Tonga I discover, to my intense annoyance, that the last nose flautist died several years ago. This was my only purpose in coming here in the first place, I must say now: to be serenaded beneath the swaying palms by the gentle rhythms of the world's only remaining practitioner of this now, alas, dead art, as the Kings of Tonga were, according to legend, lulled into wakefulness each morning by an orchestra of jolly natives, flutes up noses. And as he played, I would have sucked at a mango and thought of Gauguin. But now I learn that Gauguin lived in Tahiti. Oh well.

Still, Tonga has its attractions. Did you know, for instance, that Tonga asked to join the British Empire *of its own free will*? Well, there's weirdness, though I don't fancy Thatcher's chances of pulling the same trick with Argentina. And weirder still is this Youth for Freedom beanfeast my travelling companion is attending.

Needless to say, they wouldn't let me in, although I said I was with the delegate from Britain (who denied me churlishly), and gave the curious reason that I was too old. As most of these people, even those aged about thirteen, dress as though they're ninety, I found that one rather hard to swallow. But rejection concentrates the mind wonderfully, and so here I sit in this delightful café, content with my own company and free, once more, to lose myself in thought.

Ah yes, Thatcherism. We might do well to consider the woman who gave her name (or, significantly, her husband's name) to the phenomenon and the sub-philosophy.

In any other circumstances, she would be entirely unremarkable. A stir might be created at the WI when she high-handedly vetoes Mrs X's slide show on the boons and bugbears of jam-making to give her own opinions on immigration, but otherwise she would certainly exist in obscurity, the retired businessman's wife, occasionally joining the ranks of correspondents to 'Any Answers' and bullying her partners at bridge with her father's poisonous old opinions.

In any other circumstances? But what other circumstances could be possible? If we were to believe Thatcher's image-makers, then the destinies of Britain and Margaret Hilda Roberts are one and the same, and just as Britain was made for a new greatness (just maybe), so the Lincolnshire Gloriana was made to reveal it unto us.

And so, to get the point home, we have the grocer's shop in Grantham: the onery old pearls of grocer's shop spun wisdom remembered from when she was clanked on Alderman Roberts' knee; the tricky and mysterious metaphor concerning tea and fiscal policy; the conundrums involved in the revelation concerning half a pound of streaky bacon, two hundredweight of nutty slack and the Englishman's right to a place in the sun; and all that endless talk about Victorian values punctuating the ting of the cash register and Desmond the Dachshund on 'Toytown' on the wireless . . . And on one level it's perfect: the British political equivalent of the President's log cabin. (Interestingly enough, the last American President born in a log cabin or, more correctly, a Californian shack, was Richard Nixon, but more on this later.) However, on another level, we are also presented with a most peculiar picture of a supposedly exemplary childhood. Where, for instance, is Mother? In this uplifting tale of the Grantham girl made good, where the ghost of Father looms large as he glides ethereally between the tins of Spam and the gobstoppers, Mother seems to have been exorcized altogether – and the same goes for Margaret's sister. Where is she in the hagiography and in the misty memories of adolescent sorority, the compared acne, or little Margaret giving handy hints on the proper administration of tuppence pocket money? Questions, questions – and another to add to the list: we have the memory of the shrine in this best of all possible grocer's shops, but where is *it* now? Actually, it's now a restaurant, though what the alderman's spook must think about dissolute trendies drinking cocktails the colour of lavatory cleaner where once he dispensed wisdom about the Poor Laws as he served out haunches of snook and pounds of bullseyes must remain the speculation of the para-psychologists.

Not that his daughter must be altogether dispirited by the affluent and indifferent keeping quiet over another frosted glass of 'Sexy Stinger', even if she has to forget embarrassing facts like the failure of all that advice to produce chains of vast Roberts Hypermarkets, packed full of consumer delights and happy shoppers.

None the less, somewhere in all that are the seeds that led to the etiolated flowering of the sub-philosophy of Thatcherism – even if the final picture is mostly the work of Central Office PROs. But this doesn't explain how Thatcher came to be in a position to get her history rewritten for her; how she became leader of the Conservative Party, how she kidnapped it and now seeks to re-create it in her own image.

To understand how this has come about, we must recognize the distinct and singular quality of the Conservative Party that made it possible. It would be a mistake, for instance, to view the Party simply as a bunch of feudalist buffers who consider that they have a God-given right and duty to rule. Were that the case, we'd probably have heard the last of them with the Act of Settlement as they fled back to the Irish marches to continue their careers as highway robbers where they'd left off. There is more. Beyond the simple urge to conserve, beyond the opinion that they ought to rule (although the word 'govern' is more usually used: it sounds more principled) there is that burning commitment to ensure that they do rule, for ever and ever, and in this particular the Conservative Party has, perversely, a limitless capacity for change. Thus the original Tories, tainted with Jacobitism and with room enough in their ranks for Dean Swift, were replaced within a century by the Toryism of Wellington with its agonies over Catholic Emancipation. As the years passed, the changes came with accelerating speed, so that Castlereagh's Toryism was eclipsed by Disraeli's Conservatism, Baldwin and Chamberlain's trudging appeasement was replaced by Churchill, and the One Nation Keynsianism of Macmillan by this thing Thatcherism. To coin a phrase, one could say that the Tories operate a kind of principled opportunism. Put another way, they are fools for novelty.

And so it happened that, from the chaos of the Repeal of the Corn Laws and the fall of Peel, there arose (of all things, in the party of the grandees) a Jewish dandy as leader. With the collapse and disgrace of Chamberlain, the Conservatives did a *volte face* and turned from being the Party of Appeasement to the War Party, fell in behind the former Liberal Churchill, and have been trying ever since to pretend that the national victory over Nazism was, in fact, a purely Conservative one. We can also see this ability to change attitude with the first whiff of a different wind in the Party's treatment of its leaders: since the war (although in a very gentlemanly way, of course), they've dumped Eden after Suez, Macmillan after Profumo, Home after he lost the '64 election and Heath after he lost both the '74 elections – just as surely as they'll dump Thatcher when she loses her election.

That, however, will not be in a gentlemanly way, just as Heath's fall came about in most unseemly circumstances. For, with an eye only to the main chance, the Conservative Party has quite overlooked the loss of one of its few endearing qualities, its quaint notion of 'decency'. As many a Tory backwoodsman, snuffling miserably into his brandy as the labradors die at his feet before the family fire, might reflect: Edward can't, and Margaret can, but who is now the gentleman?

IN TRANSIT, OVER THE CAROLINE ARCHIPELAGO, 28 MAY 1985

I've fled Tonga, unswayed by the undoubted charms of Kolofuu or Fatuma, driven to despair by the massed, drunken delegates of the Freedom Binge who beset me in my café last night with their vile propositions for the abolition of all anti-drug legislation in the interests of the free market (presumably, the better to addle the wits of the electorate so that they'll vote the right way or, better still, not vote at all).

I do not care to dwell on such things, however, so instead it's off to Hong Kong, whose future concentrates the mind wonderfully.

I suppose that in 1998, when the Chinese authorities have arrested and imprisoned all the poets and intellectuals in the former colony, Countess Thatcher of Bluff Cove might shed a great, salty tear for the flotsam unfit for either of the two Chinas' ideas of free enterprise, but somehow I doubt it. Poetry doesn't seem to play too important a role in her life (Denis is certainly no Mary Wilson, although he might pretend to a knowledge of the easier bits of Kipling when the need arises), and the intellectual life she enjoys is, let us say, a distinctively personal one: bawling out Mandarins for making jolly quips in Latin one minute and staring lovingly like a moon-struck calf at Alf Sherman or Jeffrey Archer the next. Nor can I ever think of the Conservative Philosophy Group without laughing: everyone sitting around drinking bad sherry and pretending they're back in the smart set at school while listening rapt to some fruity old Cambridge don outline his plans for the privatization of the Territorial Army, or else the assembled company squeaking out a new, Thatcherite synthesis of Nietzsche's *Also Sprach Zarathustra*: 'Untermensch? Mensch? I teach you the Supermarket!'

However, we'd do well to bear these Poloniuses of the New Right in mind when thinking on Thatcher's successes. For not only is the Age of Gentlemen past in the Tory Party, but with it all the trappings of that Age. Government is no longer seen as merely a branch of estate management. The party that was once seen as requiring no more intellectual rigour than was needed to make a shooting stick stay upright now teems with all manner of wild *penseurs*; worst of all, the Party has gone professional. Thatcher is far too busy each night with her red boxes to emulate Macmillan and while away the long and empty hours reading Trollope (which she probably thinks is a kind of Warwickshire steamed pudding), and instead has turned politics into a trade. If that alone didn't alienate the traditional Tory of the old school, then her bizarre endeavours to

turn the Conservative Party of the 1980s into the Liberal Party of the 1870s must surely do so. Many an old boy, sitting and biding his time on the back benches with sad recollections of former office and his cheeks twitching as the molars grind and gnaw the loose flesh, must wonder exactly what party his Government represents.

If they were given to reflection, rather than loud hooting and a facility to pretend the immediate past never happened, the same thought might cross the Thatcherites' minds. Failing that we might consider, compare and contrast Conservatism and Thatcherism.

For some time now a large number of people have expressed concern at Mrs Thatcher's clear conviction that she is always right, but consider that from another angle. To believe that everyone else is wrong while you, alone, are right is a profoundly un-Conservative sentiment. After all, it is a central tenet of Conservatism that *everyone* is wrong, *all* of the time, and so we muddle along as best we can. Whereas socialists imagine that they can make the world a better place by relying on humankind's innate goodness, the Conservative believes strongly in original sin, in the weakness of man's nature, in the unlikelihood of his salvation, and, therefore, in the necessity for his paternal regulation. Very well, the Conservative will argue, so infants are chained to looms, old women drag carts full of coal out from the bowels of the earth, pensioners freeze to death queuing for meat they can't afford, there are millions homeless, underfed and unemployed and the cream of the nation's youth are smacked out of their heads, but what can you do about it? That's the way things are and I, for one, am not going to disturb the peace by agitating for an uncertain future, so just let them be and let me get back to sleep. Conservatism in its true sense has nothing to do with policies or conflict, but merely with conserving, with governing the existing order. The purpose of government, then, is to keep the nation ticking over, preferably in the hands of those born and educated into a position to do it with discretion, and when conflict does arise – against impertinent foreigners or the people getting above their station – then the Government's job is to keep order and to maintain the status quo.

Thatcherism, on the other hand, is completely uninterested in the status quo. It celebrates the rebirth of *laissez-faire* capitalism and glories in sub-Spenserian gibberish about the survival of the fittest, and then goes beyond this to suggest that there is a better way than the present one, that a state of nature can be created by returning to the true *laissez-faire* principles of Victorian times. Thatcher as Gladstone – which is bizarre enough in itself, but we're only just beginning here . . . Under Thatcherism, the Conservative Party, on the one hand, is the party of anarcho-capitalism, concerned with the business of getting government off the backs of the people, but, on the other, it finds itself centralizing state authority. The party of the supposed Natural Way seeks, artificially, to re-create Nature; it talks about natural levels, natural wastage, and how it is both wrong and impossible to interfere with these natural occurrences, but its creation and subsequent neglect of millions of unemployed is not a natural occurrence but a matter of policy. (The old Tories, on the other hand, would never allow such levels of unemployment as they might lead to civil disobedience.) Furthermore, as I've suggested above, in its new manifestation the 'stupid' party is alive with ideologues and born-again old Marxists like Sir Alf Sherman and Paul Johnson. Thatcherism, so busy, so impatient, so eager to change the world – and in the meantime thriving on conflict – has now introduced the Conservative Party to dialectics.

Dialectics? Isn't that what Teddy Taylor speaks with? Ah no, and Sir Alf reminds the group of the time he received the Order of Lenin (2nd class) from Comrade Molotov after his sterling work manning the machine gun in that trench in Catalonia, and points out in his dog-eared copy of *The Communist Manifesto* the opening words: 'All history hitherto is the history of class struggle . . .' Well, yes, but what a struggle, what a new synthesis as Thatcher's class, the *poujardist* petite bourgeoisie, sets about the rest. From the enemies of her first Government (the trade unions, the working class, 'the enemies within'), she then turns on the decadent aristocracy, routing the Established Church and the sentimental *padrones* in the House of Lords, and then, as the classes begin to run out, she turns on her own constituency – remember the Student Grants debacle? Thus Thatcher goes on to *épater les bourgeois* as part of her programme to achieve a suburban Utopia. Thesis? Antithesis? Synthetic!

Of course, it might not be like that at all. It might be that, rather than being weird, mutated Marxists who've crept in through the back window of Conservatism, the *arditi* of Thatcherism have adapted an older, more telling quality of Toryism and now seek to apply a vulgarized notion of the huntin', shootin' and fishin' ethic to the body politick. Extend this further, replace the hedgerows and streams of England with olive groves, the cawing of rooks with the song of cicadas, and see the gallant Darwinians as free spirits of Nature, with Thatcher as Dionysus and Keith Joseph as a rather seedy Silenus, coughing as he capers through the woods. Nature red in tooth and claw? Conflict then changes from being a by-product of the workings of the dialectic to being intrinsic to the fact of existence: pin-striped centaurs trample over the dryads to prove arcane points about 'real ambrosia for real work', unicorns are deemed unnecessary and Sir Keith, spitting out an incisor, mumbles the point again to the doubting fawns about how it's a 'Cerberus eat Cerberus' Arcadia out there.

Or is it at once even simpler and more sinister than that?

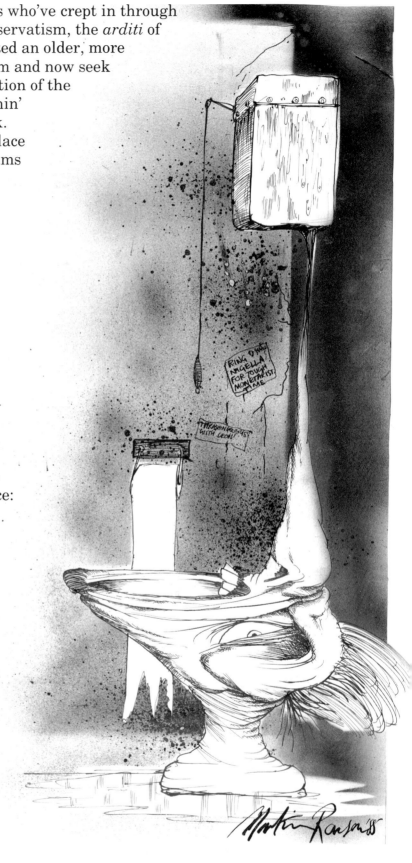

I wouldn't put it past Thatcher to believe her image-makers and see herself as much more than the Empire Loyalist factionalist with a few smart-sounding ideas that she appears to the world to be. More even than the Grantham Britannia or, as she put it in one of her Indira Gandhi moods, 'The Mother of the People'. It could be that, in wilder moments, she sees herself as The Great Purger, and we swing back to Sir Alf with his memories of the dangerous Thirties and a comforting snapshot of Stalin in every back alley cell. Thatcher, the Scourge of Capitalism?

Thatcherite Radicalism, having captured the Conservative Party for its usually docile tea-making and envelope-licking element (previously kept in check except for the annual jamboree at Conference), has let loose all the resentments and mean-spiritedness of the disinherited, deracinated but formerly deferential petite bourgeoisie, and introduced us to the politics of policy based on anecdote ('None of them wants a job! My garden gate's been broken for years and no one wants to fix it!'), rancour and vague intuition, all dressed up in hokum about the Money Supply. Could Thatcherism, then, be the revenge of that class, lashing out in all directions, at education, welfare, free health care and all the other advantages of a society it sees as having left it and its principles (hardish work, cleanliness and never speaking to your neighbours) behind? In practice, this lust for revenge is manifested by the desire to stir the buggers up and see what happens, to create a terrible internal conflict in the polity and economy, to kick them out of their sloth with a near-fatal dose of bitter salts.

Thatcher, the Enema within? Which reminds me of a kindergarten joke I heard a couple of years ago:

> Why is Margaret Thatcher like a toilet?
> They both get rid of lots of jobs . . .

PYONGYANG, NORTH KOREA, UNDATED . . .

Oh, Killane, Killane . . .
Except that the plane for Hong Kong was going to Singapore, and they wouldn't let me into Singapore because they said that my hair was too long . . .

GENEVA AIRPORT,
SWITZERLAND,
29 MAY 1985

EUROPE AGAIN, WHILE IT LASTS

A few, wild connections, and here I am, in Geneva of all places.

I vowed, long ago, never to set foot again on Swiss soil, one of the reasons being that I doubt whether they have any of the filthy stuff left these days (better to replace it with washable Astroturf in the valleys between all that clean, white snow). Hmmm. Does Thatcherism aspire towards the condition of Switzerland?

Here, after all, is a place where the inflation rate since the war has never exceeded 3%; there is practically no unemployment, and when there is you can send the jobless back to Turkey; the only riots occur when the local disco is closed down; and they've got the most efficient army in Europe, very good at the PR shots of 'our boys' yomping up mountains and digging chalets out of the snowdrifts. Moreover, the only natural dirt I've ever seen was on a sundial next to Lake Geneva, rendered unreadable by a thick layer of duck, coot and swan shit, and probably placed there as an incentive to make you go and buy a watch.

And yet I feel that Mrs Thatcher would not be entirely happy here in the land of precision. After all, half her pleasure in government seems to come from telling the shiftless, wingeing and ungrateful British to pull their socks up and that apples don't grow on trees. As with most other revolutionary movements, the Thatcherite Revolution is most fun for its protagonists in the creation; once effected, time begins to weigh heavy on their hands and then everything starts going wrong. And then there is the fact of Swiss neutrality and governmental anonymity. The second would, of course, be anathema, while the first, for all her attempts over the years to convince the rest of the world of her status as Honest Broker, would preclude the opportunity for all those photo-sessions with Ronald Reagan and those other strange little men with difficult names at EEC summits.

Still, forgetting Mrs Thatcher for the moment, Swiss neutrality does allow for some distinctly un-Swiss whackiness when Genevois venues are hired out to the latest circus to come to town. Just down the road they're still staging one of the most popular shows in Europe, back for the current season and locked behind closed doors.

I wonder what the American and Soviet negotiators are doing just now? Although there was a sense of relief when they actually got back to talking to each other about talking to each other, we still have no real idea what they're up to. Are they eyeball to eyeball over the conference table, thrashing out the terms for serious and meaningful interfacings? Or actually seeking a compromise over whose set of Travel Scrabble they're going to play with today? Even if they finally settle on the standard English version, there are bound to be problems:

'Hell, Ivan, you sure warmonger is one word?'

'Okay, Yankee, and I say "zerooption" is *two* words and it ain't in no dictionary I know!'

'You wanna bet?'

Then, the Scrabble set abandoned, these men with the future of the world held in their trembling hands glance wearily at the clock. Another seven hours to go till they can call it a day. An interpreter suggests charades.

'A book, a film *and* a warhead delivery system? You sure?'

But, oh dear, the chief Soviet negotiator gets a nosebleed trying to do Khrushchev's Secret Speech to the XXth Party Conference, so they give up on that one and opt for Trivial Pursuit instead, shuffling the packs in the interest of greater international understanding.

'What is this Babe Ruth?'

'How the hell am I meant to know who played in goal for Moscow Dynamo in 1964?'

'Plato . . . Plato . . . Hey, I know this one! It's Mickey Mouse's dog, right?'

Well, yes, and East is East, and West is West and never the twain shall meet . . .

Except that Kipling, updated from his observation of the inscrutability of the Oriental, is quite wrong. Which brings us, by a circular route, to a useful General Theory, which I call the Theory of Circular Separation and first formulated last year when a friend of mine, eager at long last to get some book learning behind him, undertook to sit a Sociology 'A' level, and was set the essay title: 'East and West are getting more and more alike all the time. Discuss.' The Theory is, indeed, universal in its application, and goes something like this: the further apart two things are, the more similar they become, and *vice versa*.

Apply this to equal degrees of beastliness in left and right wing dictatorships, and the anguished liberal is anguished no more; refer also to the common ground held between the anti-American nationalistic unilateralist armers on the right of the Conservative Party and the anti-American internationalist unilateralist disarmers on the left of the Labour Party; likewise, observe the agreement in principle between constitutionalist old buffers like Enoch Powell and Tony Benn over the Common Market, Nato and so on.

But, returning to the East/West conflict, here is an example of how the Theory works. If you take, say, Oxford Circus as the central point, at the furthest ends of a line drawn from east to west you have Washington and Moscow, cities which are almost identical. Nasty climates, gaudy public buildings, both places dominated by a secretive, remote oligarchy who speak in a strange court patois comprehensible only to their own kind and who are surrounded by slums inhabited by a disgruntled, materially deprived and cowed citizenry. Closer in, take Ipswich and Exeter. Again, pretty similar: identical shopping centres, identical ring road, similar light industries; different, perhaps, in accent, the beer they drink and the football teams they support. Then, closest in of all, take Hackney and Chelsea, which are so completely different that the native of one placed suddenly in the other will imagine he or she could be on another planet.

(It goes without saying that for the Theory to work in its geographical matrix we must assume that the world is round, which I think even the wild shamans in the Kremlin and the Pentagon do, but you never can tell. Belief in a flat earth would justify them worrying over Europe like curs over an old bone, if they saw the Bering Straits as the world's edge, dipping down into hades, and not the place for them to rattle their fancy sabres at each other.)

Another example, this time on the domestic level, is how Mrs Thatcher, a macro-conceptualist if ever there was one and a woman with an implicit faith in crass generalizations, has done her best – in the small space available to her – actually to implement the Theory and make it practice, so that, last year during the Miners' Strike, while friendly local bobbies helped fix tricycles in the leafy suburbs of the South, South Yorkshire turned into a Police State, curtailing freedom of movement, freedom of political dissent and so on. Likewise, the people of one nation have been divided into two, with the prosperous, indifferent South on the one side and the desolate North on the other. Accepting, in a moment of intellectual laxity, that the world is round, Thatcher has enabled the Third World to slip round over the Arctic and settle in the North of England.

To return to the heady matter of arms talks and the East/West divide, however, I would suggest that not only have the antagonists grown to resemble each other to the extent that it is now difficult to tell which one is which, but that, beyond that, the one is essential for the other's existence. Washington and Moscow need each other; as bogeymen with which to frighten their children, as a justification for extending their military/industrial complexes, as partners willing to observe the rules in playing their strange games. Even if President Reagan's Star Wars rhetoric about 'removing these weapons from the face of the planet' suggests the possibility of a third front opening up with the first line of defence aimed against the Klingons and the Mekon of Mekonta, down here on earth the game requires two terrestrial players to work at all. Were, for instance, the Politburo to come up with a startling initiative proposing their own immediate collective resignation followed by totally free elections, the re-introduction of capitalism and an invitation to the wrinkly Anastasia in her Kilburn bedsit to ascend the vacant throne of all the Russias, Washington would be obliged to turn it down as 'cheap propaganda'. As Chomsky has observed, for the economies of the United States or the Soviet Union to undergo any kind of growth, it is essential for them to maintain the war economy status reached during the Second World War; thus the creation and endurance of the Cold War over the last forty years, and the repeated failure of half-hearted attempts to establish 'normalcy'.

In view of this continuing state of affairs, we might ponder on the precise purpose of the latest idea for escalating the arms race, all this Star Wars nonsense. Reagan's original proposition to rid the world of nuclear weapons came with the following argument: 'If I can knock out your weapons from space' (the President wheezes, pushing jelly beans round the floor of the Oval Office) 'they just ain't gonna reach their target and do the job, are they? So there's no point in you having them in the first place. Ah, but . . .' The President gulps and continues: 'Well, shucks, I suppose if we've got one of these flying saucer gizmos you're gonna want one, too, to knock out ours.' Problems, problems, and the tucks in the Presidential forehead pucker. 'Well, I guess we could *give* you one.' But this magnanimous offer, made in Reagan's original Star Wars speech, seems to have been dropped of late, and for obvious reasons: after all, one of the main purposes in having an arms race is, with each new generation of weapons, to encourage the Russians to develop an equivalent system and pauperize themselves in the process.

The battle, after all, is not about atoms but about economics. Were those honest men locked away in the Palais des Nations to tire one day of seeing who did the best haddock impression or marking their cards before the next game of Happy Families, and instead come up with the novel idea that the whole bloody thing was costing everyone far too much money and agree to get back to the bow and arrow, the rules of the game would insist that within five years the Rockies would have been sculpted into one, vast catapult and Siberia would be filled with thousands of miles of elastic, primed behind a bigger, better arrow.

Clearly the game can go on for ever, until, that is, the point when the circumstances of the elites of Washington and Moscow finally become identical,

with both groups down in their bunkers gasping in the filtered air, and by this time my Theory works itself out, as everyone and everything is reduced to a levelling, and glowing, homogeneity.

THE PARAGON OF ANIMALS, LOWER THAN VERMIN

GENEVA AIRPORT, 31 MAY 1985

My thoughts about arms limitation are interrupted by a call from Airport Information, and at the desk I'm given a telex wiring me more money from Helen*. A brief, curt note informs me she and her children are well, but warns me to keep away from Holland Park for at least a month. She doesn't say why, but I have my suspicions. Then, just when I'm wondering where to go next, I spot my former pupil buying a copy of the *Spectator* at the news-stand and, before I can make good my escape, he buttonholes me and begins again his frightful litany.

'Wealth Creation'? 'Enterprise Culture'? What do these things mean? Thatcher's pixie looks at me with confusion but cannot tell me, but then, I suppose, in his happy faith he has no need for definitions. Just repeat the potent jujus when you wake up, sweating, from nightmares in the middle of the night, or whisper the reassuring mottoes as you walk briskly from one wine bar to the next down Notting Hill's mean streets.

At the moment I can't be bothered to work out for myself what their actual meanings may be, or may be supposed to be. Style, not content, is now the order of the day, so chant the responses and sing 'Rejoice!'

Looking at my former pupil, who just now is arguing with the woman behind the Airport Bar (in, of course, their respective languages: she doesn't understand what Malvern Water is, and he won't understand what is meant by the word Perrier), I realize that I see, personified, all that needs to be said about a certain style in today's Tory Party. There's the head, with the modishly long and tousled hair (*à la* Lawson *ou* Scruton), the chin you could plough a field with, the square, steel framed spectacles. And, inside that head, all that New Right Radical Bullshit. And, below the neck, the stripy shirt and plain, detachable collar, the thin, slightly soiled woollen tie, the old and patched tweed jacket, waistcoat and watch, fop and chain, corduroy trousers, brothel creepers ... Voilà! The Born-again Libertarian Fascist meets the Young Fogey.

Yikes!

In a simpler world, the two groups would be incompatible. The Fogeys are obsessed with the grand old rural England, horse brasses and half-timbering,

---

*Helen Killane, formerly married to Kevin Killane, author of *Towards a Methodology of Women*, etc. M.R.

John Betjeman, cricket on the green, Vicarage tea parties on dappled lawns, tally-ho for the Home Counties, fair play, *Good-bye, Mr Chips* and constant worries about the deteriorating standard of marmalade. The BALFs, on the other hand, are obsessed with 'radical reform', which presumably includes building car parks over the village greens, going for a steak and chips down the Berni Inn and not so much rewriting history (although they are both fond of and good at doing this) as forgetting it altogether in the glorious Long March towards a future of DIY warehouses, share-owning democracies, honest pay for honest labour, proper jobs, sunrise industries and the rest of the empty baggage of that philosophy.

And yet, as my former pupil so ably demonstrates in the way he presents himself to the world, incompatible they are not. While the BALFs may despise the Fogeys for being back-sliding decadents, they also secretly envy them and aspire towards their station which, for several reasons, they can never attain. Likewise, the Fogeys, apeing the sacred idle rich, are fools for perceived toughness, be it embodied by Thatcher, Bulldog Drummond, Mussolini or, indeed, Stalin. Take this further. The truly Thatcherite BALFs genuinely desire respectability, to mark them apart from the bootboys whose dicta they share, and want to know how to hold a knife properly, while the Fogeys tend to be at their most comfortable dispensing sherry on the right side of their new chums on muscle beach . . .

And as I watch this Thatcherite Fogey pocket his *Spectator* like a Bible, I think to that happy day when Thatcher will make phrenology respectable again in her Great March Backwards: then, feeling the lumps on that amazing head as the little chap lies naked, stretched out on the slab, we might be able to get behind the outward manifestation, get through the 'style' to see if there is, after all, any content, or whether the whole thing is just a pose, a new synthesis for a new generation of rebellious youth who, rejecting the liberal opinions of their parents, spurn the offered reefer over Sunday lunch, cringe with embarrassment when the Dylan records come out again, and instead choose to dress in their grandfathers' clothes and say out loud that they want to hang the trade union leaders.

And as this depressing thought occurs, my plane is suddenly announced . . .

'THE SELECT', PARIS, 2 JUNE 1985

And yet there must be more to the 'style' of Thatcherism than the peculiar opinions of certain fey young men.

But what is that style? There is a difficulty in defining it, not least because of the difficulty in defining the phenomenon of Thatcherism itself and, thereafter, that phenomenon's problem in sorting out for itself precisely what it is. As I've suggested before, Mrs Thatcher herself oscillates wildly between chosen images – and what will it be today? Wife and Mother, searching high and low through the sand dunes for Mark? or Earth Mother, plump and homely with a thousand breasts proffered to the returning cavemen? Frenzied fanatic of Supply Side screeching the truth to the unbelievers, or love-sick, dewy-eyed schoolgirl trying ever so hard to explain the simple facts to dullard media gurus?

AND YOU CAN TAKE YOUR BLOODY BIRDS WITH YOU!

THATCHER DROPS FRANCIS OF ASSISSI...

Whatever the choice, the question of style has greatly preoccupied both the smarter political commentators and a number of Thatcher's critics, including your man Pym, who clutches at straws as he attempts a definition of The Old Tory Values and, imagining himself a gentleman, denounces 'Government by Slogan' because he can't bring himself to say what he really means. Which is probably: 'This woman is a ghastly cow and I want my job back.'

That aside, her enthusiasts tell us that Thatcher's style is one of 'resolution', 'toughness' and all the other abstract nouns that tell of an inspiring ability to see and hear only what she wants to see and hear, and by the same token to be dismissive of and contemptuous towards anyone who suggests that this isn't necessarily a good thing. As far as Thatcher is concerned, this image is probably just fine, for while in psychiatric terms it is a condition which usually leads to a quiet life in a sanatorium and an endless supply of thorazine, in political terms it

ensures your place in history books and, while your luck lasts out and you aren't rumbled, an endless supply of political power. But, of course, the problem with presenting Thatcher's style as one of 'toughness' and 'resolution' is that it simply isn't true. She is stubborn, yes, which is likely as not a political advantage, but she also governs by pique, petulance and petty-mindedness, all of which, alas, aren't particularly marketable qualities for the image-makers to get to work on.

Which gets us to the nub of Thatcher's style, which is all about its language. As a piece of political rhetoric, 'The Resolute Approach' is about as meaningless as 'Ein Reich, Ein Volk, Ein Führer', and quite a long way below 'Sin? I'm agin it'. In trying to create an image about Thatcher, the PR men have, it seems inevitably, sunk to the language of bathos, and everything ends up sounding either preposterous or infantile. Thus, when the British lion had showed his long yellow teeth and chased the scrap metal merchants from South Georgia, Thatcher shouted down the curious pressmen with the stern exhortation to 'Rejoice!' or else, and to stop being silly and pretending that elected Governments are answerable for their actions. But rejoice about what? About a gamble coming off? About Mrs Thatcher saving her bacon? About her relief that John

Nott had shut up and was no longer giving the impression that the Government was in the hands of provincial estate agents? Thus a typical example of the cheapening of language.

And yet I don't think we can quite admit the language of Thatcherism to Steiner's theories of language and totalitarianism. Admittedly, a cornered minister during a rough question time may try to befuddle Parliament with so much high-sounding and meaningless bullshit (which comes somewhere near the celebrated obfuscation of the Nixon aide: 'All further references to this statement are inoperative'), but essentially the language of Thatcherism is the language of the playground. Just as we could say that Thatcherism – as the first, confused flowering of the petit-bourgeois resentment ethic – is a philosophy at best adolescent in its outlook ('Will you be my friend? No? Then take that!'), so its language is the language of taunts, threats and petulance. Mrs Thatcher may think that she is Winston Churchill, but her rhetoric hardly matches his: thus she shouts 'Frit! frit! Scaredy cat!' across the chamber of the House of Commons; calls those people who can't quite see the New Jerusalem in inner-city decay 'Moaning Minnies'; and, most notorious of all, denounces the critics of her economic policies as wets. Wets? Softies, wet-blankets, cissies, girls' blouses, too scaredy-custard to play British Bulldog with the playground toughs? Even if one can hardly imagine a phrase like 'Crypto-Keynsian running dog of *haut-bourgeois* interventionism' issuing from those ruby-red lips, in the pantheon of political abuse, this kind of thing ranks pretty low*.

*Cf: Appendix A in *Scenes from the Lives of the Great Socialists* for Killane's further thoughts on the language of abuse.

Still, I may be doing Thatcher an injustice. Her adventure playground machismo may, like so much else, be the idea of her image-makers in order to give her the common touch and make her seem approachable to the distressingly childlike electorate. And yet the evidence would seem to contradict this, for we can see the glee in Thatcher's eyes when she thinks she's come up with another stunning piece of word-wizardry. Indeed, one of the few laughs I had during the 1983 British General Election was when I heard that Thatcher was calling her campaign bus 'The Robust Bus'. What could this mean? That it cornered well? That the seats were soundly upholstered? Or that its main occupant was herself robust (you know, the old girl's worn well, still useful as a battering ram, you can bounce cricket balls off her and there's scarcely a bruise afterwards) and – magically, divinely – able to infect all about her with her own qualities?

In which case it is no wonder that, through long association, Lord Whitelaw cannot speak without producing a malapropism and that, in oratory, Michael Heseltine can come out with a fifteen-minute-long sentence without a finite verb – while, meantime, their Prime Minister bellows 'Yar boo sucks' over the barricades around her and happily elevates herself to the position of Pericles.

BAR HENRI, PORT GRIMAUD, COTE D'AZUR, 6 JUNE 1985

Now, where was I?

Ah yes, and there's a strange thing. Just now I thought I saw Hunter Thompson coming into the bar, only to be told that it was actually Gordon Liddy, the Watergate burglar and associate of Timothy Leary.

Which proves nothing in itself (and I should have remembered that poor Hunter is now beyond travel, stashed out of harm's way in his cot in the Rockies), but serves as a reminder of those wild, whacky days back in the early Seventies, when sniping at the existing structures of oppression was *fun* – or at least still exciting – and the bad guys got zapped in the end. Or so it seemed. Now, when I think of Thatcher, rather than having wild fantasies of the kind Hunter enjoyed of the ultimate retribution squad abseiling down the front of the White House in gorilla masks and carrying stun grenades, I just get depressed and, feeling incapable of doing much else, mooch off to thumb through the *Radio Times* or clean out the typewriter keys with a straightened paper clip or a piece of shattered fingernail. Which might just mean that she's won, or else that the rest of us have merely grown up.

To remain back in those heady days for a moment, though, I remember, just after Watergate broke, poor Hunter getting into a fine old bate about Nixon: 'A grim monument to everything plastic, de-sexed and non-sensual . . . When I look at Nixon's White House I have a sense of *absolute* personal alienation. The President and I seem to disagree on almost *everything* . . . Anything Nixon likes *must* be suspect. Like cottage cheese and catsup . . .' Of course, Hunter's real problem was that, beneath his disguise of Lord Weird, the Duke of Gonzo, he was just another patriotic American. When he wrote something like 'Jesus! Where

Thatcher/Nixon

will it all end? How low do you have to stoop in this country to be President?' he was *personally* affronted that anyone could be vicious and mean enough to be seen, as a matter of course, about the business of subverting the Constitution and The True American Way – particularly a small-time crook like Nixon who, as Bobby Kennedy said (and he should have known), 'represented the dark side of the American spirit'.

Of course, we can't really get away with a comparison between Thatcher and Richard Nixon. There is, after all, absolutely no evidence whatsoever that Thatcher or any of her family are in any way at all corrupt, and it would be absurd to see any similarities between, say, the Christmas bombings of Hanoi and Haiphong in 1972 and the Falklands War. Moreover, Thatcher is a completely different type of politician from Nixon, that cheap-time hustler who'd use any tactic (including, at one point, the threat of nuclear war) to retain his grasp on personal power; she is a conviction politician who will stick to her principles and philosophies come what may, and whether they work or not.

Won't she? Or will she do what the image-makers say, at the end of the day, if it's going to save her bacon? Ah yes, the image-makers, and here I'll make a modest suggestion: that Margaret Thatcher is Britain's first American Prime Minister.

What?

It's not just that Thatcher, with her capped teeth, trained voice and eyes deprived in art and life of squints, comes across as totally phoney, a packaged commodity, an adman's wet dream. There are also her origins to take into account. I've alluded above to the given perception of Thatcher as Abe Lincoln, mewling and puking in her Grantham log cabin, but we can go further. If Middle

America has a British equivalent, it is in that deracinated and reactionary, suburban lower middle class, lacking history and a sense of history, but retaining a permanent grudge, which is where Thatcher comes from and which has proved to be her most loyal constituency. All the Middle American attitudes are there: admiration for tough guys, for get up and go, for enterprise, for dream factories. And, in many ways, America – or at least the permutation of the concept of America hawked by Reagan – is Thatcher's model. She and her supporters see America as the perfection of the kind of capitalism – first developed by Britain and then adapted for human needs – which she seeks to re-create: capitalism in the raw. To this end, in a frantic search for frontiers on which to posture a frontier spirit, she's cut the nation in half, and enterprising latter-day Davy Crocketts in pin-striped buckskins venture beyond civilization up North to establish stockades in Telford. Indeed, Thatcher and her ministers are constantly wandering off to the source of their inspiration on grand junkets in search of enlightenment, for all the world like the ancient Greeks consulting the Delphic Oracle and coming away trying to make sense of the gibberish it's confided to them.

Which brings us back to 'The Enterprise Culture', a flip phrase which first gained currency after Thatcher's return from addressing Congress in February this year, and which continues to puzzle us. What can it mean? And what of 'Wealth Creation'? Simply, I think she means making money, not in the sensible way of keeping the printing presses turning, but in a new, American sense, unseen in this country since the days of Mr Gradgrind. Here we have the idea, moreover, the philosophy, not of making money towards any particular end, but, in the context of unbridled capitalism, of *making money as its own end*. Imagine it! Vast continents of krugerrands, palaces of swag, and let them suck bank notes!

Mindful of the American influence, Thatcher outlined her plans recently in an interesting variation on another piece of rhetoric when she told us that she, too, had a dream: a dream of creating a nation of capitalists, a share-owning democracy. Which is just dandy if you discount about half or more of the population who will never have the opportunity to sprout share certificate wings and fly away to this fiscal never-never-land. But the dream persists, expands and soon engulfs all, despite the fact that there is, according to Norman Tebbit, a media conspiracy to show the 'Wealth Creators' as scheming sharks when we all know (or should do, if we know what's good for us) that these people are kindly philanthropists busy about the grand task of saving the nation. Where will it all end? Are there, even now, gnomic figures in the dungeons of the Centre for Policy Studies rewriting Dickens? But we gotta go further! Total purgation! Tear it down and build it up again, a whole brand-spanking-new society of noble wealth creators sucking quails' eggs over another strenuous business lunch while up and down the land the happy treadmills are alive with the sounds of hymns sung to the Brave New World of profit and loss and free market competition!

There is, however, a problem with trying to turn Britain into a nation made up of the nastier characters from 'Dallas'. Although Thatcher and the Thatcherites

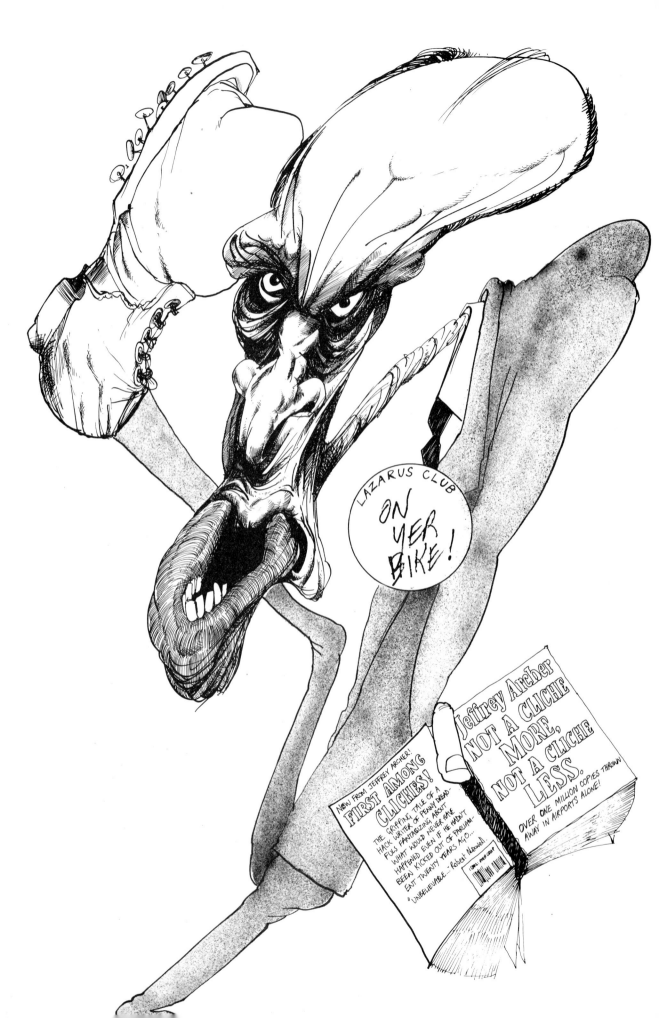

should not be expected to see this, there is something wrong with that philosophy which puts a better pension plan as the height of cultural endeavour; which would gladly make a bonfire of all the paintings of the Renaissance if the choice was between that and visiting the MFI Warehouse on Sunday afternoons; which seeks to create a society where you exile the poets the better to enable you to read the British Telecom Shares Prospectus in peace.

To what extent Thatcher has made Britain the 51st state in Reagan's America I cannot say. Certainly, for a number of people, the wild dash to privatization does, amazingly enough, constitute an adventure of sorts (wrestle them bears! cross them ravines! read that deposit account super savers statement!). And yet, in the exodus to find the Shopper's Promised Megamarket, something seems to have gone awry. It is a fact that, rather than being a heightened spiritual experience – you know, you walking into Safeways and a voice of thunder booming from Heaven to send you, instead, to salvation and cheaper fish fingers in Sainsbury's – shopping makes most people really grumpy, and this is because it is *boring*.

Which fact Thatcher seems incapable of recognizing. Although I should not, perhaps, extend the idea of Thatcher as American Prime Minister too far, I cannot escape the impression that there is something in Thatcherism that translates the Kerouac fantasy into burning rubber across a continent in order to buy a hamburger; and, moreover, something in her image, her presentation and her packaging that has little to do with British politics, but equally not enough with American politics to make it viable. There is a dream, but it is the dream of the sleep-walker, or the comatose, and that dream is ultimately small-minded, bathetic, tacky and boring boring boring. No amount of seduction by the propagandists will ever succeed in convincing me that the small businessman setting up an electronics factory in Milton Keynes is today's answer to the wild frontiersman, to Sir Francis Drake, Neil Armstrong and Spartacus all rolled into one, and that all human desires are met when the people reach the condition where they are free to do nothing else except fall asleep in front of their television sets watching 'Dynasty', dreaming about cheaper double glazing and the golden opportunities for all the family in swamp-land developments east of the Surrey docks.

BRITISH TELECOM PROSPECTUS

JOIN OUR GREAT ADVENTURE!

There is, I recognize, the problem that a significant number of people may actually wish to nod off into a coma in Thatcher's sedative Utopia. Indeed, it is one of her triumphs that she has changed the ground rules for the Class War, embourgeoising a large enough constituency docile and self-interested enough to allow her to say to hell with the rest. But it's Thatcher's problem that she has to make such a lot of noise in lulling the population to sleep, so much that they occasionally stir enough to notice that the local hospital has been turned into a rollerdisco, that the refuse collection franchise has been sold to the Kray Gang and that the pavements are now under two-foot of grass – with luck that clamour may be her final undoing.

I reflect on this as I visit the cemetery island of San Michele to spit on Ezra Pound's grave, and muse on what happens when you put monetary considerations above all others, as when the news of the Doge's death was kept secret for two months rather than spoil the end of the tourist season. Shortly afterwards, the Serene Republic was besieged by Napoleon's armies and the 800-year-old state collapsed in about half an hour, voted into extinction by its fearful merchants.

Well, that's one way of dealing with things like that, although somehow I can't see Thatcher going in the same way. So what is there left to do? Draw up socialist Blue Books cataloguing the crimes? Arm the claimants? Sell the *Socialist Worker* down the shopping centre on Saturday mornings and wait for the State to tremble to its very foundations?

I'm not sure how far we can go in comparing Venice in its decadence with Britain today, although in one consideration at least they may be similar: decadence is usually marked by a growing collective boredom, which itself spawns a general enthusiasm for novelty, just because it's different and makes a change. Thus, Venice had its ever-more-spectacular carnivals, and the population was diverted by ever-more-spectacular freak shows touring Italy and thrilling the sensation-hungry Venetians with their geeks; and Britain has Thatcherism.

What? The Thatcher Government as a Freak Show?

Marvel at the Iron Lady! Gasp at Nigel and Leon, the fattest fatties in the World! Thrill at Norman, the wildman of Chingford, thirty men brave and true lost in his capture! Wonder at the brain-dead Foreign Secretary! Roll up! Roll up!

And then, when you've paid your dime and ogled at the stars, visit the listless ranks of grey golems in the back tents: why, here's Nicolas Ridley and, yes madam, drive your hatpin into the fleshy part of his thigh! See, not a flicker! No feeling at all! The games go on and on. Ask the Secretary of State for Education the simplest question and see him tear literal chunks of flesh from the barely living body as he puzzles out the answer! Kick Patrick Jenkin in the crotch and see him wonder if you're being witty or not! Gasp and giggle as Norman Fowler tries to say 'rabbit' without sounding like Elmer Fudd! Ask Tom King about unemployment and squeal with disbelief as he repeats, robot-like, that we're well on the road to recovery!

Of course, this is no more than an unintentional by-product of Thatcherism. We're meant to believe that our rulers are principled, honourable, talented men to whom we should be grateful for taking our destiny in their hands. Unfortunately, what the world sees is a shambling bunch of talentless, time-serving no-hopers trying to put a brave face on it without looking too hag-ridden. And while it might be fun to sneer at their physical freakishness, we'd do well to remember that the ugliest parts of their bodies are their minds.

Take a man like Sir Keith Joseph, a Secretary of State for Education who doesn't believe in education. On one level we might feel sorry for poor Sir Keith, who apparently hasn't said a word in Cabinet for a year and a half now and just sits looking anguished and sucking his hanky; but we should be wary, and remember that this is the man who, in his office at the Centre for Policy Studies, was discovered one day shivering in the terrible cold, staring mournfully at the electric fire moaning 'it doesn't work; it's broken; why is it broken?' until someone obligingly plugged it in for him, and who's often been seen in the corridors of the Palace of Westminster fretfully banging his head against the wall. It is typical of the attitudes of this Government, moreover, that when it became clear that Joseph was totally unfit to continue running the Department of Trade and Industry, rather than packing the old foamer off to a nursing home, Thatcher remembered that this was her Svengali, the brilliant man who'd first filled her head with all that mesmeric balderdash about money supply. There was no way she could exile him from her Government, so instead, for occupational therapy, she pushed him off to Education, and never mind he knew nothing about education, for here he could amuse himself to his heart's content, planning to re-introduce teaching of the phlogiston theory to the 'O' level Chemistry syllabus, babbling wildly to the teachers that it was their fault they earned so little because they were teachers, and out of harm's way. Education is, after all, of no consequence whatsoever to the Thatcherite Grand Plan.

And then there's Patrick Jenkin, the archetypal sacrificial lamb whose blandness and incompetence just serve to add insult to injury as his minions at the Department of the Environment set about the destruction of local government and the centralization of power. But, again, there is this terrible urge to pity. It was, after all, Jenkin who, during the 1973 Miners' Strike, suggested the people share their baths while his London house was photographed by a man from the *Observer* with every light in the place burning. Does he really know what he's doing? Or is he just led, dribbling and smiling idiotically, to his desk each morning and set the task of trying to remember as much of his civil servants' brief as possible before Question Time in the Commons without either falling over or getting a biro caught up his nose?

And what of Geoffrey Howe who, as Chancellor of the Exchequer, succeeded in losing his trousers on a railway train and seemed capable of even falling asleep

For Anna *junior by far* × × × Martin Rowson '93

himself during one of his speeches? Now, according to the pundits, he's making rather a good job of it at the Foreign Office, but this is not too difficult, the secret being to do absolutely nothing and wait and see what happens, and then to release a statement. Of course, he's helped to apparent success by Thatcher's celebrated hatred for the Foreign Office: being her placeman he's seen, for some reason or other, as a focus for quiet opposition and common sense as he dozes off during banquets given for the Dalai Lama.

But these men occupy offices of state Thatcher considers, at best, peripheral to the dream; the plum jobs are kept for her creatures. In this respect, at least, Joseph, Jenkin and Howe look the part: gibbering, cowed or just plain vacant, they have the look of men who have been through some frightful experience and lived – just – to tell the tale to an unbelieving world. Thatcher's creatures, with whom she consolidated her position at the start of her second term, do not have this look. They don't need it; they *are* that frightful experience, incubi from Thatcher's Hell of Mediocrity.

Ah yes, 'let me have about me men that are fat' . . . Safe men who don't think too much, or who are willing to suspend thought and judgement. For, of Thatcher's inner circle, this is the difference between men like the Normans

PATRICK JENKIN sticks hard at his desk, administering the nation with ability and courage...

Fowler and Tebbit and men like Leon Brittan and Nigel Lawson: Fowler and Tebbit jabber away without making much sense, but give the impression that they actually believe in what they are trying to say, whereas Lawson and Brittan are seen almost universally as apparatchik toadies, immeasurably smug and pompous and quite prepared to say almost anything at all so long as it doesn't get them yelled at by the Prime Minister. Indeed, so amazed are some people by the present attitudes of Lawson and Brittan, Thatcher's Kamenev and Zinoviev, which are the precise opposites of what they previously advocated, that a theory has grown up that they are playing a waiting game, appearing to be rabid Thatcherites so they can sneak interventionism or liberalism in through the back door of the Cabinet.

This seems to me to be unduly generous towards these fat goons, whom I cannot see without thinking of those other fat politicians: Mayor Daley, Robert Muldoon, Herman Goering and Idi Amin.

But were these men lithe Valentinos it wouldn't make much difference. As I suggested above, there is a moral ugliness that cannot be disguised, that makes Leon Brittan sweat and smarm on TV, not believing a word of what he's saying while he closes down gay bookshops, fills the prisons to bursting point, hands supreme power over to the police and thinks of the best way to deport refugees and molest Asian women at the airports; that makes Nigel Lawson choke and stammer in the House of Commons as his economic strategy collapses around him and he babbles wildly, desperately, about the need for a 'no-tech' economy, trying to remember the riddles he learnt at Reagan's Oracle.

Paragon of the animals? Or lower than vermin? For there are two distinct pictures of Thatcher's Government: the one, which most people can see for themselves, of the incompetent in pursuit of the impossible; the other, the picture the image-makers would have us see. Frantically remoulding the model, they keep telling us what a kindly, thoughtful, gentle woman Thatcher is, how delightful and witty her colleagues. Why, she writes letters to her retired retainers, can show such consideration, and, when things get a little too much (as they must in so strenuous and important a job), she has a little cry on Denis's shoulder. (And presumably rubs the streaks of rust off her cheeks with a brillo pad afterwards.) You know things are getting really desperate when we start getting fed this kind of tear-jerking *Woman's Own* twaddle. Ah yes, but that's it, and part of the Thatcher dream: a cosy middle class *Woman's Own* world where the Prime Minister is wife and mother and exemplar of all the feminine virtues; where, if she were not herself so remarkable and invaluable to the future of the nation, she would lead the women of Britain by her own example back to the kitchen sink. Meanwhile Carol writes rubbishy books (or, as she might say, 'wather cwappy'), and the society pages are filled with photos of the chinless, debutante daughters of Cabinet Ministers dancing the night away at the Berkeley Square Charity Ball.

Well, I suppose if I had any decency in me I'd be mightily impressed by these glittering young imbeciles and feel really sorry for poor Mrs Thatcher, the cares of the world on her frail shoulders. As it is, I prefer to concentrate my attention on more important things, and keep my sympathy for some of the victims.

Talking of whom, I seem to have left someone out. Yes, that's it, which leads us nicely to . . .

'REJOICE!' or THE POX BRITANNICA

PORT STANLEY, EAST
FALKLAND, 11 JUNE 1985

God, this is a dreadful place . . .

I'd forgotten, since I was last here, just how dreadful it was, although recent events have probably made its aspect, if possible, worse. And all this frantic travel has addled my mind to such a point that I overlooked the fact that what might pass as reasonable dress for the season in Venice is hopelessly inadequate to match the fierceness of the Southern Winter.

Ducking out of the blizzard into the Upland Goose, I ask after the kelp trader from whom I bought a walrus (unseen) here in 1978. The walrus never arrived, and any inquiries about the man elicit nothing but dark grumblings about 'dang Argy lovers' and that "e's moved away', and then silence. I order whisky, am given instead a pale, tasteless libation called, mysteriously, Penguin Ale, and so retire to a nook by the fire to muse on my lot.

I've always had a fondness for walruses, although why *Trichecus rosmarus* should have captured my fancy as it has so many other people's is a mystery. It's due mostly, I'd suggest, to the whiskers and the tusks, and, while wishing to avoid the pitfalls of anthropomorphism, I'd return to my earlier theme and say a lot of these beasts bear a marked resemblance to Lord Thorneycroft (despite that latter's signal lack of tusk, etc). Why I wanted a walrus for my zoo in Camden has little to do with cuteness, however. It was my original plan, on founding the place, to pre-empt the times and differ from most other zoos in creating little eco-systems for the creatures: cobras and mongooses, spiders and wasps, that kind of thing. Having read Captain Gray's log of the S. S. *Eclipse* for 6 July 1879, in which he describes a sea battle between a walrus and, of all things, a narwhal – 'The walrus was in prime condition. The blubber upon him was three inches thick; his stomach was quite full of pieces of sealskin and the part of the narwhal which he had eaten. He had, at a moderate estimate, one hundred and fifty gallons of oil and blubber in his stomach' – I toyed with the idea of pulling in the crowds by re-enacting this titanic conflict, nature red in horn and tusk, and so on. Ah me, such wild flights of fancy – I should have known it would come to nothing. Live narwhals are almost impossible to come by these days (the only one I saw, in St Paul's Bay, was actually a *Pseudorca crassidens* with what looked like a pool cue stuck crudely to its snout), but I was so enthralled by the idea that, tortuously, I made my way to the Falklands to see this trader, who promised me so much and delivered nothing. I have since learned that walruses live exclusively in the Northern latitudes, and this present trip, taken on a whim when I suddenly remembered my absent walrus as I was sitting in Harry's Bar, was to settle the score.

Well, yes. Settling scores and absent friends. That seems to sum up the Falklands pretty well; then and, even more so, now. Then, in 1978, the place seemed to have practically nothing to offer: Brunel's 'Great Britain' had been towed back to Bristol some years earlier, and beyond the sheep, the seabirds and a few dour crofters here and there, there was nothing of any consequence at all. The same could, in a jaundiced moment, be said today, except that it isn't true: the population has quadrupled at least, the calm of the galeswept uplands is disturbed at regular intervals by the silly sheep foolishly grazing in the minefields, and the consequences seem countless.

The greatest single consequence had its second anniversary just this last Sunday, which seems to have passed unnoticed: perhaps Thatcher sees her 1983

Election victory as nothing more than par for the course, the kind of unremarkable event you encounter every day between rubbing shoulders with presidents and laughing politely at diplomats' jokes which you don't understand. Kicking my heels on Ascension, I declined joining a drunken major in wild toasts from his hip flask to mark the occasion, but I wonder, now, if anyone joined him.

What, for instance, was Thatcher herself doing? Was she too busy to pay heed to the witless Gummer's stuttering panegyrics comparing her to St Theresa of Avila, and half-heartedly comparing herself to St John of the Cross? Or was she, devotee of the older religion, sparing half an hour to read the Tarot with Laurens van der Post before returning to the weightier matter of the medal to mark Cecil's return to the fold? Cecil? Oh, Cecil – perhaps she sees the anniversary in a completely different light: a dreadful mistake, marking the time when her luck started to run out and the banana skins fell like the very raindrops from the

heavens; when, although she'd managed to kick out the jams, things started going mysteriously, terribly, tragically wrong ... She should have had some prescience of it when the choirs started singing out in Downing Street as she idly doodled on the curt note giving Pym the push; should have known it couldn't be this easy – and then Cecil sidled in, lower lip trembling, and in the next moment he was sobbing uncontrollably in her lap, pulling at her stockings as he unfolded the terrible story of his shame. Oh yes, how bitterly she regrets that day, shudders at the memory of it ... her most trusted lieutenant compromised, a horrible foretaste of the coming Nemesis, and she could kick herself for listening to those fools from Saatchis when she should have just called in the Army all along. After all, it'd worked before, hadn't it?

What? Paranoia this soon?

But the Falklands 'conflict' invites paranoia and conspiracy theories of all

kinds, whether they be about the *Belgrano* sinking, the amazing good luck of a winnable Imperialistic war being dumped in Thatcher's lap just as her popularity was reaching its nadir, or the fact that, of the War Cabinet of Nott, Parkinson, Pym, Whitelaw and Thatcher, only Thatcher remains. What can it all mean?

Indeed, what can any of it mean?

I always thought that the best justification for the Falklands War came from a dotty old dietician who pointed out that the Argentines simply couldn't have the islands and their population because of the difference between the diets of the two peoples. The scheming gaucho lives on nothing but raw beef, which ruins his digestion, while the plucky kelpers dine on old mutton and seaweed, resulting in them being among the most regular of Her Majesty's subjects. The prospect of garlicky miasmata clouding the kitchens of Puerto Argentino or a thousand Argy settlers overburdening the already inadequate Port Stanley sewers with the stinky consequences of their culture shock was so ghastly that war became inevitable.

Could that be it, then? That this was the first Health Foods War, with 'our boys' yomping to glory over the sphagnum marshes chewing mouthfuls of bran,

Colonel H. being callously cut down by the podgy Argies as he selflessly offered them a bowl of muesli, Admiral 'Sandy' Woodward mumbling 'I see no sheep' as he panned the horizon and tucked into a plate full of curly kale, washed down with fresh orange juice? It makes as much sense as anything else.

There was, after all, no real need to send the Task Force. The Islanders themselves would have been happy enough to go to New Zealand with two grand each in their smocks to husband their scrawny flocks elsewhere, and snoozy, sentimental memories of the *Pax Britannica* don't seem to have played much part in defending the interests of Hong Kong, the Bananan Islands, Grenada and other lands where the Queen reigns as Sovereign. There was certainly no policy of opposing fascist dictatorships anywhere at all, so we can hardly account Thatcher's desire to see the overthrow of the *junta* as her justification. There was, possibly, the need for Britain to have some presence in the South Atlantic, against the day when the Panama Canal silts up or as a base for the krill trawlers when the last cow plods into extinction. But even then, the Islands had been protected much more effectively only a few years previously when a Labour Government, bothering to pay attention to the intelligence that the Argentines were about to invade, put them off by sending a couple of Polaris submarines down there.

But none of this takes into account the thinking of the Prime Minister, that fine political acumen, that toughness, that resolution. The scene, then, is this: the Defence Staff, having received certain intelligence from the South Atlantic, has an audience with the Prime Minister . . .

PM: Well, what is it?
DS: We have information that they're about to invade the Falklands.
PM: The Falklands? What's that?
DS: They are some islands we own in the South Atlantic.
PM: Really? That's nice. And who are 'they'?
DS: The Argentines, Prime Minister.
PM: The Argentinians, eh? Aren't they that lot in the bottom left hand corner run by that tough and resolute bastion against Communism? Whatsisname, Galtieri? The chap we sell all our old weapons to?
DS: That's right, Prime Minister.
PM: Well?
DS: Well, we . . . er . . . that is, some of us were wondering what you were going to do about it.
PM: Do about it? What do you want me to do about it?
DS: Well, um . . . we thought, ah, as they were about to invade . . .
PM: Just a minute. Cecil!
CP: Yep?
PM: How are we doing in the polls, Cecil?
CP: Piss awful, Margaret.
PM: I see. Well, you ask me what I'm going to do about it. We're not going to do anything about it. We're going to have a war.
DS: Gosh! Thanks, Ma'am!

Spooks, Goons, Bozos, Creeps and Other Matters of National Security

Enough is enough, and I've got to get out.

The Falkland Islanders are bad enough themselves – strange, unfriendly beings, more like H. P. Lovecraft throwbacks than anything else, who live here precisely because they despise the company of people and want to be left alone to interbreed on their blasted heaths – but it's the new, itinerant population I can no longer endure. So far I've been vomited over by a drunken squaddy, almost beaten up by drunken construction workers, propositioned by drunken journalists and implored to buy a bag of fish and chips by a confused Empire Loyalist couple barely subsisting in a caravan on the outskirts of town, so I await the next plane out, whenever that may be, spurning offers from the wily natives of a rowing boat trip to Tierra del Fuego.

I appreciate that the little scenario I concocted yesterday may strike some people as unlikely, but here we begin to meet the problems: half the things you want to know about the Falklands War are covered by 'National Security' and the other half don't make any sense in the asking. Why, for instance, did Thatcher's 'War Cabinet' include the Chairman of the Conservative Party? What does Cecil Parkinson know about the conduct of wars beyond, obviously, what is and what is not politically acceptable and just how many corpses you can build your election hustings from? Moreover, as I mentioned earlier, why have all these people disappeared from public office, either retiring, sacked, disgraced or dumped upstairs in the House of Lords? Did they witness Thatcher chewing the Axminster once too often? And then there's the matter of Thatcher's surprise visit to the Islands in January 1983: since when has a Prime Minister been empowered to present medals to members of his or her Monarch's armed services, whose loyalty is to the Crown and the Crown alone? Questions, questions, and all the answers are secrets.

Indeed, with the web of secrecy that's been woven around the whole conduct of the Falklands War, can we even be certain that it took place at all? A war conducted in secret, reported under strict Government control by a sympathetic media, where at all costs those who know or suspect the truth must be got out of the way (either removed from public office or else sent off to vast tracts of MOD land in Scotland under the codename 'guarding the Falklands') – who's to say it really happened as they claim?

But here we really are letting the conspiracy theories run wild, when really the 'National Security' dimension is quite simply explained, even if we're not allowed to talk about it. So, although everybody knows it, we're not allowed to say that the Americans did all the surveillance work for the British during the war, because if we did we'd get them into all sorts of trouble with the Organization of American States – which is no way to treat an old and valued ally. The only trouble with pretending that no one knows this is that the Government has then got to make sure that nobody knows anything else either, so everyone can continue to pretend that nobody knows anything about anything anywhere ever. Thus Tam Dalyell, the Ponting Trial, the GCHQ Union Ban, the proliferation of theories about the truth behind the sinking of the *Belgrano* and all the rest.

I am now convinced that that truth, at least, is a simple one: the *Belgrano* was there and 'our boys' on the *Conqueror* wanted something to do. But you can dress this up any number of ways: bloodlust in the 'War Cabinet', the urge to scupper the peace plan, breakdown in communications, or whatever. That the *Conqueror* was not justified in being in a position to fire the torpedoes in the first place is another matter altogether, but it might just explain the whole *Belgrano* business. You can imagine it. Down in the bunker the first reports crackle in over the ether, and the 'War Cabinet' goes berserk. 'Gotcha!' they scream, cracking open the bottles of pomagne and breaking into the crate of party hats, but then . . . the first seeds of doubt. My God! We'll never get away with this! Anguished look meets anguished look as one by one they each see a terrible vision of the future: War Crimes trials, massive proliferation as a shocked and horrified world runs to the aid of plucky little Argentina, a massive defeat at the polls . . . Then Thatcher comes to one of those resolute, statesmanlike decisions for which she is justly famed all over the planet: 'Boys,' she hisses through clenched teeth, 'we gotta lie about this one . . .'

Ah, but one lie leads to another, and soon there are so many lies, told in an effort to confuse those nosy defeatists who doubt the Government's word, that in the end the Government is the most confused of all. But, having made that first move into mendacity there's no going back.

And all in the name of 'National Security'. But there are problems there too: 'National Security' against whom? All potential enemies know all the secrets anyway, which is why they have spy satellites, moles in the MOD and all the other bizarre paraphernalia of international relations. In this light, 'National Security' is just another of those meaningless phrases like 'actions incompatible with one's status as a diplomat'. One of the main functions of a diplomat is to find out what's going on in the host country, and, similarly, 'National Security' has nothing to do with external enemies. It's all about the enemy within.

It is a long-held Establishment assumption, upheld by Tory and Labour Governments alike, that Britain's greatest enemy is her own population – all of it – who, ungrateful wretches, are always disturbing the peace of their rulers. In this way of thinking, the wishes of the islanders are never paramount (except maybe at election time, and only then if they have the wit to vote the right way): they must be protected from themselves, told as little as possible and put in prison if they make too much noise or let too many cats out of too many bags. Thus it is a question of 'National Security' that the British people must not know too much about what went on in the Falklands War – just as a matter of principle – and anyone, like Clive Ponting, who tries to tell them anything must be put in prison (although in this case, things never being as they seem, it appears that Ponting's motive was actually to get at the Armed Forces Minister, John Stanley, a minister whose civil servants are rumoured not to have been sorry to

see the back of each time he lumbered into another department and who also once said that Britain doesn't deserve a leader like Mrs Thatcher – which is getting interestingly close to the attitude of those Soviet scientists who wanted to re-name the moon 'Stalin'). Similarly, if someone like Sarah Tisdall tries to tell the British people when the weapons that are going to defend their way of life are due to be installed, then she too must be put in prison.

Cute, eh? But, unfortunately, Governments get into problems with paranoia too, particularly this one with its bunker mentality and its ever longer list of enemies within. I mean, who can you trust?

Clearly, anyone on the left is a threat to national security (instance the furore when the former Chief Constable of Devon and Cornwall shredded the Special Branch files on people who'd had meals with Tony Benn) and so, too, is anyone associated with the Peace Movement. But who else? Can you trust anyone?

Two Cautionary Tales, then.

The first one involves the cartoonist Rowson's father, an amiable old doctor of independent opinions who is also, of course, a member of the National Trust. A couple of years ago the Trust decided to sell some meadows it owned to the Ministry of Defence, that they might build a nuclear bunker beneath them. Not surprisingly, certain elements in the grassroots membership of the Trust objected to their organization, set up in order to conserve the British countryside, dealing with people who were even then involved in schemes that might result in that countryside being blown to bits. These radicals called an Extraordinary General Meeting of the Trust to discuss the matter, which was held at the Wembley Conference Centre. Rowson *père* attended this meeting, and as he walked up the steps of the Conference Centre, surrounded by typical members of the Trust – ex-officer corps anglers in tweeds with tackle in their hats; large, billowy lady water colourists from Hampshire – he noticed, down a side street, three busloads of riot police, waiting for the inevitable. Clearly the Council of the Trust, seeing the hand of Pacifism in this opposition to their plans, were fully expecting an attempted overthrow of civilization; could see the mob, their smocks smeared with blood, wielding chintz cushion covers stuffed with cobble stones and pouring down a rain of Beatrix Potter figurines and pots of homemade chutney onto the heads of the beleaguered upholders of law and order. The enemy within? You betcha!

The second story is even more bizarre, and concerns Lord Lewin, the former Chief of Defence Staff. Some months ago, the Serious Crimes Squad went round to Admiral Lewin's place. But what could they be after? Was the real secret about the *Belgrano* about to be revealed to a waiting world? That the bugger wasn't sunk at all, but that Lewin had *stolen* it (he had motive, opportunity, a highly trained and unswervingly loyal gang to do the dirty deed) and buried it in his back garden to gloat over in the long years of his retirement, while bewildered Argentine sailors roamed the Suffolk countryside? Alas, the truth was at once much more mundane and, characteristically of the Thatcher Government, cack-handed. Lewin had given an interview to two journalists from the *Guardian* in which he'd mentioned certain matters still classified, thus quite clearly contravening Section II of the Official Secrets Act . . .

Dear God! You know things are getting pretty desperate when they even begin to think about chucking the man who won them their bloody war in the first place in the slammer.

. . . AND THEY SAID THAT DEATH SHALL HAVE NO DOMINION . . .

HOTEL DUVALIER,
PORT AU PRINCE, HAITI,
14 JUNE 1985

I speak of paranoia, but this is ridiculous. This disagreeable fascist rabbit appears to be trailing me like a hungry dingo.

Luckily, this time I saw my former pupil coming first and was able to duck out of sight, watching the wall as he went by, deep in conversation with a large official in dark glasses I took to be the Haitian Minister of the Interior or some other such placeman, although what this much-travelled Thatcherite elf is doing here I daren't even begin to guess. No doubt it's some grisly fact-finding mission *à la* Alf Sherman, so he can scuttle back to the Kitchen Cabinet ('Which Cuppa-soup for you, Ma'am?' 'I take the anchovy and bromide, thank you') with hot news about Haiti's 'major advances on human rights', happy tales about the operation of the free market in this 'bulwark against Communism' and some handy hints on Voodoo for Sir Keith . . .

Grim, grim, and to my shame I escape into drunkenness with my friend Zeitlyn, the anthropologist, here doing some last-minute research for our book*, and together we sought the midnight company of the gorilla. (You know, that unperceived and understood gorilla who in the middle of the night creeps into your room while you're asleep, throws your clothes on the floor, sicks up over your trousers, gobs in your mouth and hits you over the head with an iron bar.) This morning, then, I keep to my bed and the security of the rum bottle, and in this fallen state I mix my metaphors and, suitably enough, ponder on the State of the World.

Despite what I may have said in Port Stanley, I do not personally subscribe to the Conspiracy Theory of History, but instead to the Cock-up Theory (a view I share, apparently, with Bernard Ingham, the Prime Minister's Press Secretary, even though I do not believe this man to exist). Along with the Cock-up Theory go the Accidental Theory, the Serendipity Theory, and so forth. Thus, one school of thought when looking at, say, the Storming of the Winter Palace, will say that it is the result of the successful politicization of cadres of the army and proletariat, financed by Jewish bankers' gold, whereas I prefer to remember that the Winter Palace was stormed on Trotsky's 38th birthday. (The scene is a low bar off Nevsky Prospect, Trotsky and Stalin eyeball to eyeball over a sea of empty glasses: 'Okay, Josif Vissarionovich,' hisses Trotsky, the party hat falling crazily over his pince-nez, 'I betcha a crate of vodka that me an' the boys can overthrow the Provisional Government jus' like *that*!' Trotsky tries to click his fingers a few times while Stalin narrows his eyes. 'Okay then, Lev Davidovich, you're on!' The rest, as they say, is history.) The only problem with subscribing to the Cock-up Theory comes when you consider those people who advocate the Conspiracy Theory, many of whom are sufficiently monomaniacal to ensure they get into positions where they can go about the business of setting up conspiracies to their hearts' content, usually to counter other conspiracies seen either with deranged zealotry or crude cynicism. Thus we've had the Jewish-Bolshevik, Trotsky-Bukharin and International Communist conspiracies, which don't and didn't exist, and a thousand and one others, intrigued in the cells and rumpus rooms of the CIA, KGB, MI5, Society of Jesus, the Freemasons, etc. which surely do and will exist. Ah me, and take your places for another round of the Great Game.

I talked about the East/West Conflict earlier, but thinking about it still boggles the mind, as Al Haig so eloquently phrased it. Reagan furiously supports tyrannies (or, as Mrs Jeanne Kirkpatrick would say, reminding one of adverts for French lessons in a Fifties copy of *Men Only*, 'disciplinarian Governments') whose only policy is the systematic genocide of their compatriots, while democratic and popular Governments that aren't to Reagan's, the Pentagon's or the State Department's taste are subverted and overthrown. Meanwhile, the operatives of the CIA toil in their laboratories to perfect the elixir which will finally make Fidel Castro's beard fall out so he'll lose his charisma (this is true,

---

Archaeology and Anthropology in Hollywood: From 'The Mummy's Curse' to 'Raiders of the Lost Ark', Blackwells, 1985

and they haven't found it yet), KGB gunsels strap another peace activist's genitals to yet another car battery, and the public officers in the client states of both sides set about the torture, mutilation and murder of their citizenry.

Still, in order to keep sane in this madhouse, where the maddest inmates are capering among the filing cabinets in Admin. and fiddling with the dials on the ECT machine down in Correction, we might consider some options. Why, for instance, this terrible enmity between the United States and Iran? It would appear to me that here, surely, are the most natural of allies, and if only Jerry Falwell and the Ayatollah Khomeini could bring themselves to get together through the offices of the Ecumenical Movement, they'd confound humankind. After all, the opinions of the Moral Majority in America and the Fundamentalist Moslems of Iran are almost identical: subjugating women, hanging homosexuals, crucifying Communists, stoning to death anyone who entertains any ideas formulated after, say, 500 BC – and all in the name of God! Indestructible. Likewise, why hasn't Mrs Thatcher asked that nice General Jaruzelski to give lectures on union bashing at Sandhurst? And, while we're pursuing this vein, I'm reminded of an idea Judith Hart shared with the late James Cameron at the time of the Iranian Hostage Crisis, just after Carter had announced the American boycott of the Moscow Olympics. It went something like this: the Soviet Army withdraws entirely from Afghanistan and instead invades Iran, topples the mullahs, liberates the hostages and flies them back to Kennedy Airport, first class Aeroflot with Georgian champagne and caviar all the way, and then sits back to wait and see what Carter does about it.

Dreams, all dreams, even though they've made me feel a little better, although that could just be the rum.

To return to the business in hand, then. While my former pupil is no doubt inspecting the guard of honour provided by the *Tonton Macoutes*, thinking what a fine body of men they are and turning a blind eye to the peasants starving in the fields, we might turn our minds to Britain's role in this Great Game.

Why, I wonder, does Britain continue to kid herself that she still counts for something in the world outside, that knavish foreigners still tremble in their disgusting huts when the lion roars and that (the greatest piece of self-delusion) she is an equal partner with the United States in the Defence of the West, the Free World, the Democratic Way of Life and the other clichés that seem comforting when Britain's lost another Test series to the Bangladeshis and the national pride's wearing a bit thin? It is time, I would have thought, to wake up to the fact that she is a third-rate power that may be good at winning little wars against fourth-rate powers but tends to look rather foolish dragging her independent nuclear capacity up Whitehall in a shoe box and elbowing frantically for a place at the Superpowers' table.

But, of course, in Thatcher's Golden Time no one's going to admit to uncomfortable truths like those, particularly when such an admission might compromise that essential state secret which no one's even begun to guess at, that Thatcher's entire foreign and defence policy (with the possible exception of Grenada, when the Queen got tetchy about her Caribbean subjects) is dictated, slowly, from Washington. And the time has now come for me to fill a gap I left

during my reflections in Venice and deal with the man who presents this policy; deal with the matter of the Defence Secretary.*

In spite of the porcine delights of Leon Brittan or Nigel Lawson, the thrills and chills of Norman Tebbit, the *sans-culotte* charms of Norman Fowler, even the dubious but earnest enchantments of the Prime Minister herself, I have to admit that the Cabinet Minister I despise the most is Michael Heseltine. It is difficult to say precisely why I hold this opinion, but there is something about the man – the mixture of glamourpuss, smart alec and whizz kid – that I find offensive and repellent. You can imagine him in the kindergarten with a basket of apples for teacher, a three-foot-long box of *Caran d'Ache* crayons, a full collection of football cards all in order in his scrapbook in its neat, clingfilm jacket, and with an infinitely smug expression on his face when he excludes you from his gang in the playground. But more than this, I feel that in his smugness he has nothing at all to be smug about beyond the fact that he feels he's just done something terribly, terribly clever, like swinging the Mace of the House of Commons round

*Since this section was transcribed and illustrated, Michael Heseltine has ceased to be Defence Secretary. For Dr Killane's thoughts on Heseltine's resignation, see the Appendix at the back of this book. (Editor's note, January 1986.)

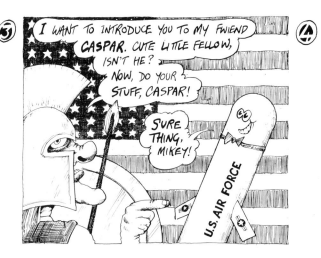

his head and waiting for the applause, or eating a Mars Bar sideways to amazed and admiring oohs and aahs. Which might explain why he enjoys himself so much as Secretary of State for Defence, where he can play soldiers to his heart's content, dress up in uniforms and cut the dashing beau with his flowing locks and his vanity, oblivious of the fact that to all the world he appears the buffoon and, without really trying, has succeeded in turning himself into Mrs Thatcher's Herman Goering.

For there is a strange story behind Heseltine's elevation to this office of State, in which he plays no active part but which involves two important facts of political life.

The first is that the post of Defence Secretary is the Russian Front of Cabinet appointments. The job, essentially, is impossible – trying to arbitrate between the rival services, abandon another part of Empire in good order or get the Ordnance factories to make bullets to fit the guns – and taking it on has marked the end of many a promising career. (The only exception to this rule is Denis Healey, who was, apparently, just too good to be kept down; other, more recent incumbents include John Nott, that 'here today, gone tomorrow' politician, and Bill Rodgers. Who?)

The second important fact of political life has less to do with government, and more to do with the Conservative Party, and is that Margaret Thatcher's single greatest political enemy is Michael Heseltine. And so, on Nott's resignation, Thatcher, mindful of these facts, put two and two together, and came to a nice conclusion: Michael was perfect for the job! If the position itself didn't finish him off, then a few nasty surprises in the near future would: the arrival of Cruise, the purchase of the ever-more-expensive Trident, plus all those gory-locked ghosts from the Falklands who refused to rest in peace – all of which he would try to explain to Parliament with deliciously embarrassing bombast while not understanding a word of what he said. And I think Thatcher may, for once, have made the right decision. Can anybody ever take the Victor of Molesworth seriously again?

But there is an official version, of course, which is that Heseltine was given Defence in order to deal once and for all with CND, those unwitting dupes of Moscow who, however much MOD loot is poured into the Wives' and Mothers' Wine and Cheese Whist Drives for Peace and Security and other witting dupes of Washington, still seem to keep on winning the argument. This, typically, didn't seem to worry Michael or anyone else in the Government, and they all grandly declared that the Peace Movement was wrong, slandered it mercilessly during the '83 Election Campaign, declared just as grandly afterwards that it was dead and took to locking up its supporters instead. (Speaking of slander, I remember a particularly fine piece of nonsense from the philandering Great White Heap Cecil Parkinson, delivered just before the election and his disgrace to a pack of the party faithful who wished to know no better. Speaking of the Labour Party's new unilateralist stand, he said that this was just the continuation of a fifty-year history of 'Labour appeasing dictators'. But of course! And in the cafés of Catalonia the old men still talk of the gallantry with which the Neville Chamberlain Brigade fought for the Republican cause and Lord Halifax helped set up the Fourth International.)

But can we entirely blame Heseltine for his actions? I suspect that before he became Defence Secretary he'd never heard of CND, and what can one say of a man, drunk on his own tortuous rhetoric, who can say to the Conservative Conference: 'I personally guarantee that there will never be another Labour Government!' Is there something he knows that we don't, or does he just want to be loved? Indeed, there are moments when I can almost begin to feel sorry for him, before I take hold of myself and return to my wits. There is something rather pathetic about the poor fellow, who only wants to please and who thinks Mrs Thatcher is being a bit rough on the deserving poor, standing up in the House of Commons and fumbling, with complete incomprehension, through the gibberish his civil servants have given him to read and then – oh calamity! – having to think on his feet when a tricky and unforeseen question comes up. As when, for instance, announcing the arrival of Cruise at Greenham Common, he admitted (did he know what he said? was it all a ghastly dream?) that American servicemen might easily have to shoot some of the Greenham women if they got a bit close to the silos.

Which suggests an interesting moral and intellectual puzzler: are you justified in killing peaceful protestors protesting against a weapon for which you say the main justification is that it safeguards a way of life where the people consider it their greatest liberty to be able to engage in peaceful protest?

Problems, problems, and they won't go away. For instance, Heseltine tells us that we may sleep soundly at night in our beds, that Britain's Defence Strategy is based on deterrence, and that we'll never use these filthy weapons so it's all right, really. But then Mrs Thatcher, discarding her Earth Mother or Queen Empress image, one day decides to put on the hat with the television aerial and play at being Supreme Leader of the Treen Intergalactic Battle Fleet and declares that she'd be quite happy to press the button first. So Michael has to try to patch up his PR and peddle the deterrence line all over again. But, if what he claims is true, why are these things locked away behind miles and miles of barbed wire and guarded day and night by foreign soldiers armed to the teeth? If they are integral to the preservation of the British Way of Life, and aren't going to be used anyway (unless, that is, we think *they* think that we think they might fire a few off), why isn't there a cruise missile on every village green, carved with friezes depicting scenes from Britain's Island History and doubling as maypoles when required? And if you think that that's taking things a little too far, what about this? Why is it that those people who want to remove the army and weapons of a foreign and potentially unfriendly power from their country's sovereign soil are dubbed as traitors, while those who want that army to stay and are happy to have their country's foreign policy dictated by that alien power consider themselves patriots?

I suppose the answer is that it's all part of the Great Game, which is beyond our understanding. There is no point in asking 'Why?', because the participants in the game won't understand you and are intellectually incapable of reaching the simple conclusion that life would be simpler and safer if everyone dispensed with the damned things if no one was going to use them anyway.

Still, we might conclude by speculating on an unconventional future move in the Game.

Assume Britain disarms unilaterally, and the Muscovite hordes swarm across Europe and invade the sceptred isle before the Americans get a chance to reclaim their lost largest aircraft carrier. Would anyone be able to tell the difference? You never know, it might be an improvement; some people might prefer a cultural imperialism that brought the Bolshoi ballet, real vodka and cheap Beluga caviar to one that has already brought Coca-Cola, McDonalds hamburgers and 'The "A" Team', and doubtless the bureaucracy would much prefer dachas in the country and special shops to the constant hectoring of Mrs Thatcher. But then, of course, they'd start installing the SS20s . . .

NO ARTS, NO CULTURE

Right, keep moving.

I've been listening back to my reflections of the last few weeks with dismay: clearly I was getting in a bad, bad way, sounding more and more like a fatal combination of bar bore and Vaudeville Cobber, using idioms I thought I'd expelled from my vocabulary decades ago. This is disturbing. What's happened to my celebrated analytical powers, the arch and arcane prose style, the deft juggling of idea and theory? A telex from Dexter Jakes, to whom I sent the first tapes of this oral travelogue, implies that my mind is getting addled by too much travel, done too quickly, and perhaps he's right. It is, after all, a savage old lie that travel broadens the mind; on the contrary, it narrows and calcifies it, and the further the traveller travels, the more he or she can think only of a warm bed and the comforts of home. Time for repose, then, on the S. S. *Caliban*.

But before I settle down to my ease, a final thought on the Nuclear Issue. I recall a bizarre theory I first heard from a one-time neighbour of mine, a biker known only as 'Freebase Kevin', which, in its implications, surpasses even the notorious Havana-Tel-Aviv-Teheran-Vatican Conspiracy for calculating evil. It was Freebase's opinion that Governments possess nuclear weapons not to defend themselves from other Governments, but for purely aggressive purposes aimed against their own people – the enemy within. In short, at a stroke, they could rid themselves of those teeming millions of obstructive citizens who ceaselessly hamper the business of smooth government, and, after the radio-active dust has settled, these cynical tyrants would break out and up into a perfect, if rather barren, world. The only problem with this theory, of course, is that, on emerging from their bunkers into the glowing Arcadia, the politicians, bureaucrats and figureheads would all be devoured on the spot by the few remaining sick and degenerated survivors, delighted at this sudden and fortuitous supply of fresh and uncontaminated meat.

But enough of these depressing speculations. I've been exploring my cabin and have found many interesting things. A pair of suede shoes that fit me, some pipe tobacco, several golf balls, a three-month-old copy of the *Observer*, a novel by Martin Amis called *Money*, a half-full bottle of bourbon – the discarded effects of previous passengers. I put on the shoes, blow the tobacco around the table top, throw the golf balls out of the porthole and settle down to read the *Observer*, drink the bourbon and make little paper aeroplanes out of Amis's penny dreadful.

And now here's a thing: my old mate Clive James reviewing feature films, translated to video tape, for those readers who've forgotten the original reviews written elsewhere by less gifted hands. Not that I expect Clive would remember me as we last met when he was three and I was five, in Jannali where he'd come to visit his auntie, and all I remember is him running off in tears when I shoved the runt into a billabong. Well, he's certainly no runt these days, and makes a sort of living putting stupid captions to photographs in the colour supplements, and seeking a reputation for himself as poet, novelist, critic, autobiographer and *belle lettrist* in succeeding slim and successfully unreadable volumes in his chosen genres. And all this from an original career sneering, in his own thick Strine, at the funny way foreigners talk. And yet, together with Amis, Craig Raine, Julian Barnes and the other glitterati of liberal education I now care to forget, little Jamesy appears to have instituted a sort of Scriblerus Club for the Thatcher Age, where these giants of contemporary letters crack dirty jokes to each other, qualifying each *canard* before the giggling's subsided by mentioning Rilke, and dreaming of having dinner with Alexander Solzhenitsyn who, if he bothered to turn up, would probably suck meanly at his black bread and exhort them, in Church Slavonic, to mend their ways and seek the ascetic life.

What? Am I implying that, through the TV column of the *Observer*, these latter-day Addisons and Steeles define the literary age in writing praise of Thatcher's Great Anna? Of course not, for that has been left to daft old fogeys like A. N. Wilson, Amis *père* and Philip Larkin (and if only he'd become Poet Laureate: 'they fuck you up, the King and Queen . . .'). Rather, it's that they are typical, indeed symptomatic, of a time that allowed Thatcher to be possible, and, as Madox Brown said of Rossetti, that they end up seeking salvation along the course of least resistance. After all, if you wish to impress your audience by appearing to perform your tasks effortlessly, then it's obviously best to undertake tasks that involve the least effort.

Is this entirely fair? After all, these people do try terribly hard, whether it's Jamesy trying to be a Renaissance man while kidding himself he hasn't been rumbled yet by his indulgent audience, or cute little Martin Amis trying to play the pretty boy thug so he won't be patted on the head, dressed up in a sailor suit and asked to recite 'The Wreck of the Hesperus', or even Bill Buford trying to forget that he was once the drummer with the rock group 'King Crimson'.*

But what, then, of the cultural life of Thatcher's Britain?

---

*I think Dr Killane is getting confused here between Bill Buford and Bill Buford, who is, of course, someone completely different. M. R.

I've observed elsewhere that Thatcher and the Thatcherites, with their obsession for the high aesthetic of the money supply, would gladly exile the poets and, by their very natures, will always prefer an evening in watching 'The Two Ronnies' to a night at the opera. Moreover, quite apart from the embarrassed posturings of poor Grey Gowrie trying, like Cromwell in tweeds and a natty bow tie, to close down the theatres, I wonder whether Thatcher and her closest lieutenants even really know what is meant by 'culture'. Rather than reaching for their revolvers, they might be thinking greedily of petrie dishes and the antiseptic delights of the stinks lab and reaching for their spoons . . .

Which at least means we might be spared a new Thatcher Aesthetic, a weird Capitalist version of Socialist Realism, with paintings hung in the Royal Academy of Thatcher holding hands with laughing children by the gleaming flanks of spanking new hydro-electric dams. But, considering this, we should not forget that new mood, that Thatcherite climate, where there is a subtler process at work. Cut art subsidies, certainly, and leave it to Teddy Taylor to call for all expressions of anti-Government sentiment to be banned, but the society itself will do the rest of the work for you, so that even highly praised attempts at analysing and criticizing Thatcherism, like the film 'The Ploughman's Lunch', end up less a criticism and more a symptom, and 'satire' like *Private Eye* sinks back to the level of blowing raspberries at teacher, persecuting the harmless (like gays, women, blacks) and a populist obscurantism.

> NOW THAT EVEN MUGGERIDGE DOESN'T THINK THE A.I.D.S. JOKE'S FUNNY ANY MORE, CLEARLY THE TIME HAS COME FOR ME TO, UM, DIE...

A new frivolousness is abroad, which on one level explains *Private Eye*'s current success (why, it's now even sold in W. H. Smith, which Richard Ingrams often said would mark its final absorption into 'The Establishment'), and on another is best observed in the sociological substrata, in the youth cultures. I have written at length elsewhere about these phenomena*, but consider this: less than ten years ago a new and briefly dominant culture arose with the Punks, but where are they now? True, younger sisters and brothers still pour glue over their hair and rip their clothes, but to what end? The originators of the movement were expressing a nihilism among certain young people who felt vaguely alienated from a quite stagnant society, and so expressed themselves,

*In *Mao and Marcuse: The Gerontocracy of the New Left*, Seven Seas, 1968, and *The Moon and Napalm: Journeys to a Free Saigon*, Random House, 1976.

inarticulately but magnificently, by banging their angry heads against a cardboard wall. The political climate now, under Thatcher, is quite different: she advocates policies in the manner of a crusade, and whereas Callaghanism (the term coins itself uneasily; the phenomenon hardly existed at all) presented nothing to rebel against except an amorphous sense of stagnation, Thatcherism is a fortress ripe for besieging and storming. But what has happened? There is opposition, certainly, but no dominant youth movement to articulate that opposition. Many young people, having been deemed surplus to requirement in Thatcher's vision of the Better Britain, have internalized their despair and sought comfort in self-destruction. Otherwise, market forces dominate: no longer do students sit around endlessly discussing the latest situationalist fly-sheet, but instead either work through the night in the libraries and fret about their grant or sit around debating how much Crème de Cacao to pour into their cocktails. Otherwise, the young brood about vegetarianism while their boyfriends fuss about their clothes, which eyeshadow to wear and how fat they're getting. Meanwhile, the chic radicals of the smarter inner city ghettoes divert their energies to seeking a revolutionary synthesis through film reviews, and, God spare us – and *how* did this happen? – the Hippy revival continues apace. And even when they do man the barricades, as first happened in 1981, rather than making the final push to set up the Toxteth Soviet, after a while they move off to pick up a few videos or TV sets from the smashed shop windows in an effort, through whatever means, to join Thatcher's consumer paradise.

Ah yes, style without content, and the journalist-anthropologists divide and subdivide the children into their neat, orderly and quite harmless classifications: Yuppies, Sloanes, Mods, New Romantics, Young Fogeys, etc., all linked not by a common goal but by a common self interest and self obsession. Meanwhile, the 'Soccer Hooligans' smash up the stadia and murder each other, the civilian manifestation of the spirit of 'our boys' who were washed to heroism on the crest of the wave of the New Imperialism.

In that respect, at least, Thatcher has not been entirely successful in creating a new British militarism, even though I find something very disagreeable about this celebration of 'our boys', whether they be the strapping scum of the earth fit for the victory parades or else the glorious fallen. (The ones in between, the surviving wounded, are not, however, pleasing, and must be kept out of sight and soon forgotten.) I covered the homo-erotic, sado-masochistic dimension of warfare – the wholesale slaughter of beautiful young men – at length in my book *The Moon and Napalm*, particularly with reference to the Vietnam War and the anti-War movement, but I think in the aftermath of the Falklands war we see the first thin flowering of a strain of the phenomenon helped, no doubt, by the yellow press.

Ah yes, the press – a pause for thought . . . Here, at least, there is neither content nor style. What more can one say?

Some advice, then, for when everything seems too much and the dark melancholia threatens to descend and reduce one to bleak inaction, when you feel the veins and arteries begin to clog up with the bodily wastes and the mind begins to fill with slurry. You can clear the head and free the passage of the blood by sluicing a healthy dose of adrenalin through the system, and you achieve this thusly: spend ten minutes thinking about Sir David English, Kelvin McKenzie, Sir Larry Lamb, Andrew Neil. The mere thought of these mendacious, pompous, time-serving hacks is enough to heighten you to a fine old rage and inspire you to action. With the moral scruples of wolverines, the courage of wombats, the intellectual rigour of opossums and the self-righteousness of terrapins, these dingbats serve in this regard at least.

And as the times prescribe frivolousness, I might as well share an idea I've had for some time of playing these people at their own game; of starting up a low tabloid with the one purpose of exposing and inventing stories about Fleet Street journalists. Imagine, if you can, the joy the following headline might bring to an otherwise lacklustre day: 'Daily Mail Editor Eats Babies for Breakfast. Exclusive Pictures Centre Pages.' Or else: 'Sun Man Reveals "I Cannot Read or Write!" Sobbing uncontrollably, Sun Editor Kelvin McKenzie told amazed colleagues during a top-level editorial meeting this a.m. that he is "totally illiterate". Continuing, bronzed Sun supremo and former postboy Kelvin, 25, explained why the Sun is always full of total lies: "I'm not responsible. How am I meant to know what these things say? Personally, I blame the media." Kelvin's boss, Australian zillionaire publisher Rupert Murdoch, commented from his Bavarian mountain fastness: "This makes no difference. I have total faith in my editor."' And on and on we could go – at least it might make a change from this endless balderdash about the Princess of Wales's latest brand of toothpaste or hairgel.

Which, somehow or other, brings me to another recurrent fantasy.

Although I find it by no means a privilege, I remain, through some historical trick, a subject of the British Crown, but then again it's so long since I had anything to do with Australian politics that I haven't exactly done much to alter this state of affairs. But I remain of the opinion that, however harmless the individuals may be, the institution of monarchy, with its mummery, its patronage, its systems of honours and the rest of that dangerous nonsense, prevents any kind of radical change from taking place in Britain while it remains in place. In short, the monarchy is the cock crowing atop the dungheap. But, saying this, I realize that it will be quite impossible to get rid of the monarchy because, simply, the press wouldn't let you: it is essential to their subtle subjugation of the people, a vital ingredient in the ceaseless potage of palliatives dished out by the Establishment press every day to keep the citizens quiet: bread and circuses. So, in 1981, through the worst breakdown in public order for fifty or more years, the glittering pomp of the Royal Wedding kept the bulk of the people glued to their TV sets and off the streets. (Merseyside Police went one step further, celebrating the Royal Wedding *and* the International Year of the Disabled in one go when they ran over and killed a man on crutches going home to watch the fireworks by driving from one riot to another up a backstreet at sixty miles an hour without lights.) And while the proles are kept in check as the real news is exiled to the bottom of page four, and the nation holds its breath as Princess Margaret lights another gasper, Princess Anne falls off another horse or Princess Di turns up at Henley in a lurex binliner, the individuals, as people,

disappear altogether, and become mere symbols, characters in an up-market soap opera.

To return to my fantasy, then. Were I grudgingly obliged to accept the old old argument that the monarchy is a necessary institution, a constitutional safety catch, the court of last appeal (oh yeah? and look what happened to Michael Fagan, who thought his Monarch could sort out his problems and was put in the madhouse for his naïvety), I would say, in spite of their dehumanization, there is still the problem of the people involved. They cost an inordinate amount of money, and cannot always be relied upon to keep in their place: thus the Duke of Windsor flirting with fascism, the Duke of Edinburgh mouthing off about unemployment, Prince Charles giving everyone the benefit of his architectural wisdom, or even the Princess of Wales getting moony when she meets pop stars in public. Why then, the answer is simple! We now have the technology to dispense with the people altogether, while maintaining the institution! All that need be done is construct a vast computer of precious metals, inlaid with fabulous gems, built on casters that it may be dragged up and down the realm on royal progresses, fitted with crafty holes from which champagne bottles can be fired at ships to be launched, programmed with twenty-five simple clichés to feed out in random order on any given occasion, and outfitted, on top, with a metronome, bearing a single white glove, that it might wave at its loyal subjects as it bleeps and whirrs about its regal business.

But, as I say, the press would never let you get away with it, and I feel the Royals themselves might be rather reluctant to give up all that loot and publicity to go off and run riding stables, pubs or hairdressing salons.

Perhaps that's it, and we've finally arrived at Hesse's feuilletonistic age, where the highest form of literary expression is journalism – worse still, bad journalism – and Britain's whole cultural life has taken a jolt and sunk down a notch. The yellow press, at the bottom, sinks lower; the quality press embraces bingo for the smart set; the critics, novelists, intellectuals, sink to the level previously held by the quality press, and, as is the nature of things in this 'natural world' where market forces operate, everything reaches an equilibrium to suit the times, Mrs Thatcher's Times.

A MAD WORLD, MY MASTERS . . .

THE ELM TREE,
CAMBRIDGE, ENGLAND,
2 JULY 1985

Back in Blighty, and a 'phone call to Helen gets me the answering machine with a strict message that Holland Park is still out of bounds, so instead here I am in the Fens to meet with Rowson, who doesn't show.[1]

I've never liked Cambridge, although I've had cause to visit here often, whether on academic junkets from UEA or when I spent a miserable sabbatical here doing research for my book on Sykes-Wolsey[2], fruitlessly tracking down witness to the friendships he avowed in his diaries – with the likes of Richards, Empson and Jennings, for which I could find no evidence whatsoever. I cannot add to what I said in that book, expressing both my own frustration and disgust and Sykes-Wolsey's attitude to town, University, College:

> To this end the very structures of Cambridge, the fount of those stimuli, must be found wanting: King's Chapel is unimpressive for the period: a failed fertility symbol, unconvincing upturned sow whose teats, erect and turned mortar, are directed, both futilely and blasphemously, to the Heavens and away from the lean farrow. Likewise, 'The Backs', indicative perhaps of the ephemeral nature of all existence, are poor metaphor: systemized, sanitized, damp but unwelcoming, green but spiritually pallid. And so it is with all these famous 'sights' in Cambridge. Trinity Great Court? A bourgeois and soulless experiment in symmetry that emerges, in terms of any sensible behaviourist continuum, asymmetrical if purely by virtue, or lack of it, of the impotent symbolism of the flaccidly phallic fountain; King's Parade? Consumer capitalist thoroughfare, no serpent in Eden, a mere slow worm slithering towards bathos; Pembroke College? Guano-streaked aberration, throw-back to the shabby practice and performance of the Countess's agents in the Black Death, vile, low, dwarfism manifest . . .

My thoughts about Sykes-Wolsey have now undergone a complete reversal, but my opinions on Cambridge remain: are, if anything, reinforced.

---

1. In fact, on this particular evening I was where Killane had arranged for us to meet, in a pub called the Free Press ten yards down the road from the Elm Tree. M. R.
2. *The Lost Vortecist: A Biography of Julian Sykes-Wolsey*, OUP, 1978.

Of course, it's meant to be part of the charm of places like this that they never change: the centuries unfurl and countless generations of gilded youth pass through, but the place itself – moreover, the spirit of the place – endures untouched. Even so, in the eight years since I was last here, certain things have changed and, naturally, for the worse. In 1977 there was still a last, faintly glowing ember of the student radicalism of the Sixties and early Seventies, and the dons maintained their fortress mentality, quivering with fear and loathing into their port, or else practising tentative collaboration by playing Bob Dylan records in lectures or cautiously skinning up a jay at faculty parties; now, however, things are quite different. The reactionary and trendy dons survive, certainly, but now most of the students – or at least those who look up from their interfaces long enough to dwell on such matters – would probably agree with all of what the reactionary dons say. Indeed, that dreadful Brideshead programme has done its foul work, and the *jeunesse dorée* mince from cocktail lounge to wine bar and then set off in pursuit of their beagles. As to the dons themselves, their ranks are now swollen by ever more doyens of the New Right, Thatcherism's shock troops.

These are the true Thatcherites, more Thatcherite than Thatcher herself; the Born-again Libertarian Fascists who provide a sort of intellectual basis for Thatcherism – from the tittering *fin de siècle* roués of the Cambridge Senior Parlours, who seem to have learnt all their history from Visconti's 'The Damned', to their chums who have moved beyond the College to spread the glad word in the *Salisbury Review*, the Centre for Policy Studies, the Adam Smith Institute, the *Journal of Economic Affairs* and other trend-setting groups and periodicals of wow-now modish reactionary thought. And if we ask, in the words of the old Glaswegian taunt, What are they on? Who are their mates?, we'll see that here, rather than the traditional High Tory Common Room buffers, are children of the petite bourgeoisie eager to rewrite their personal histories and disguise the occasional wayward vowel intonation, people with a tendency towards Anglo-Catholicism who like getting sniffy about Victorian churches. And as is *de rigueur* for the best of them, many are converts, men of passion who cut their teeth opposing the Vietnam War or polishing their Marxist pose in the glint of the riot shield, and who now attach themselves to what they conceive to be a greater revolution by far. With earnest talk of 'libertarianism', they plot the privatization of everything, everywhere, and kow-tow at this proud fetish as the first step towards their salvation.

Well, I suppose the privatization of the police force does have some attractions – the convenience of having all crime committed and investigated by a single body, the maintenance of public order dependent on who pays the most; likewise, the notion of privatizing the Army can't be faulted for originality or, indeed, an almost intoxicating whackiness.

But of course, the impression they wish to create of themselves is not of devil-may-care zanies caught up in Dionysiac frenzies, but of stunningly clever and serious men of immeasurable *gravitas*, concerned with the destiny and welfare of mankind. So it's a shame, in a way, that, like everything else to do with Thatcherism, they end up looking plain dumb. Take, for instance, *The*

Omega Project, a sort of anatomy of Britain job some of these people thought up. We must assume the authors spent many hours fretting over a title that would give the correct impression of seriousness, importance and eschatalogical profundity; unfortunately, they've ended up with something that sounds like a Jeffrey Archer spy thriller. And this is inevitable. Paul Johnson may howl and paw the ground and scribble panegyrics about suburbia and the tidy decencies of the middle classes, and Roger Scruton may decide he's the cleverest man on Earth and feel that thrill of sensual excitement shifting in his loins when Nicolas Ridley squeaks about the great adventure of deregulating bus services, but these people have never overcome the original problem that, as I've suggested above at length, *capitalism just isn't very interesting*. Except, that is, when it's in crisis, which seems to be most of the time.

Still, these frightful people continue to bleat about 'freedom', the freedom to starve, the freedom to be exploited, unemployed, deported (if you're the wrong colour), blown up (if you're the wrong nationality), hanged, imprisoned (if you espouse the wrong cause) and all the other freedoms essential for a just society. (Or, to put it another way, just about a society.) And these pin-striped Ché Guevaras of the New Right, these smooth Nechaevs of Anarcho-capitalism, high on half-conceived theories about individualism, are besotted (for all the world like the archetypal, stereotypical Marxist) with the weird rites and ancient magic of economic theory.

Ah yes, economic theory. It's always so much easier in theory.

The two people I hated the most when I was at Chicago were, perversely enough, Milton Friedman and Herbert Marcuse: the former because he was so

unpleasant about a rather complimentary book I wrote about him[1], the latter for other, more personal reasons which also eventually took book form[2]. Nowadays, Marcuse is almost entirely forgotten, the one-dimensional man has turned sideways and disappeared altogether from view. Friedman, on the other hand . . .

Here is neither the time nor the place to discuss at length the theories of monetarism, and I will content myself with a handy piece of backchat I thought up a few years ago. You know, when you're at some dreadful party and a young exec. finally realizes that you're a socialist. 'Ah yes,' he'll say, 'that's all very well in theory . . .' To which you must immediately rejoin, 'As opposed to monetarism, which doesn't even work in theory!' To this extent at least Friedmanite monetarism qualifies perfectly for the pantheon of intellectual Thatcherism, with Milt and Mrs F. desperately fiddling their figures to make them match their conclusions, just as hapless Secretaries of State fiddle the unemployment and job vacancy figures (down 300,000 in the first instance, up the same amount in the second) and the Thatcherite gurus busy themselves rewriting history.

You can't entirely blame them for their mendacity: it's not so much wicked-ness as the terrible need to fit the facts to the figures, to attempt the creation of a make-believe world where, if nowhere else, the policies make sense. A cosy world where bozos like Patrick Minford, the Dr Strangelove of Liverpool University, can argue that the unemployed aren't suffering enough yet to make them want a job (and it's nice to see you again too, Mr Bentham), so you must cut their benefit to make low-paid drudgery 'attractive'. 'Unavoidably, it would reduce the income of the previously lowest-paid unemployed; this is an unhappy side-effect . . .'[3] 'Attractive'? 'Unhappy side-effect'? This is middling grade 'A' level Economics, low-grade 'O' level English. And while the Goneril Professor Minford was forecasting in March 1981 that the then present levels of unem-ployment would result in no social unrest[4] (one assumes he was out of Liverpool that summer), presumably elsewhere in the Institute of Economic Affairs people were hard at work calculating the exact date of the Coming of the Beast.

And yet, for all their fine ideas, monetarists are like spiders, Christians and Communists: they despise and devour one another. Incapable of settling on a commonly held version of the 'truth', they cannot agree with each other on anything except on one issue, and that is that Thatcherism has gone badly wrong and so, independently but inexorably, the rats have been leaving the sinking ship more or less since it was launched. Friedman went with Thatcher's first budget, when Geoffrey Howe increased VAT to 15% and inflation to 24%; Waters and Hayek have distanced themselves from the whole frightful mess; David Laidler, once one of Thatcher's most influential economic advisers, was writing about 'Botched Monetarism' as early as January 1982[5].

1. *The Dialectics of Monetarism*, Chicago, 1966.
2. *Mao and Marcuse: The Gerontocracy of the New Left*, Seven Seas, 1968 (see also 'Herbert Marcuse: The One-Dimensional Man Plays with His Ideological Cut-Outs', *New Left Review*, August 1968).
3. *Journal of Economic Affairs*, Vol. 3, No. 2, January 1983.
4. *Quarterly Economic Bulletin*, March 1981.
5. *Journal of Economic Affairs*, Vol. 2, No. 2, January 1982.

That Margaret Thatcher is not General Pinochet is probably a cause for regret to both her and the monetarists, and in view of this wanton oversight it's hardly surprising that she's been hamstrung: no chance to shoot the trade union leaders, no opportunity to carry out social terrorism unchecked by that vulgar fear of the wrath of the electorate; no freedom to lock up your opponents so that the economic experiments can be continued uninterrupted. But there remains the central question which the monetarists, safely back in their university departments or economic institutes (count those krugerrands, boys!), have chosen not to confront: have they disowned Thatcher because her Government has been 'wet' and has fallen by the wayside on the path to righteousness, or because, in implementing their policies, she's proved them to be unworkable? Monetarists are, after all, human beings too, and humankind cannot bear too much reality, especially when it gets in the way of neat ideas.

For Thatcher's economic policy has been a complete fiasco. The growth in output from 1979–81 was smaller than in any other three-year period in sixty years, and this was with the support of North Sea Oil. Essentially, the economy has been, at best, standing still; at worst, going backwards. As to the control of the money supply (M3), the touchstone of monetarism, compare the periods April 1976 (after the IMF visit) to October 1979, under Labour, and June 1979 to April 1982, under Thatcher:

Period	Target (%)	Out-turn (%)
April 1976–April 1977	9–13	7.7
April 1977–April 1978	9–13	16.0
April 1978–April 1979	8–12	10.9
October 1978–October 1979	8–12	13.3
Total for Labour	33–51	47.5
June 1979–April 1980	7–11	10.3
June 1979–October 1980	7–11	17.8
February 1980–April 1981	7–11	22.2
April 1981–April 1982	6–10	13.5
Total for Tories	19–32	47.8 (approx. calculation)[1]

In other words, after two and three-quarter years of strict monetarism, the Tories managed to increase £M3 by about 48%, slightly more, in a shorter time, than Labour, *and* with lower targets! Hence Thatcher managed to plunge the economy into its deepest recession in fifty years *without* cutting the rate of growth in the money supply! No wonder the shamans of monetarism were impressed. But still those who remained had their misgivings: they have been thankful from 1982 onwards that inflation has begun to fall, but still wonder, rather helplessly, when there's going to be any real growth in GDP. By 1983 North Sea Oil had brought the GDP back to the 1979 level, but 'Production and Construction' – in other words, where the jobs are – was still down 6%. Unable to

1. This table was received with the package containing the Cambridge tapes, scribbled on the back of a cigarette packet. M. R.

see the real culprit in their own philosophies, loyal monetarists like Minford sought a scapegoat and found one (surprise, surprise) in the unions, just as in the 1930s, despite the fact that Thatcher's battle against the unions (essentially an ideological rather than an economic one) had been effectively won.

On an intellectual level one might, if pressed, have a grudging respect for Thatcher's policies if they were callous but efficient; as it is, they are callous and inefficient, to the point where now no serious academic will even begin to try to justify them. It's well known that Thatcher herself never knew what she was talking about, and just made an effort to remember what her marketing managers had told her, but at least she once had men about her who could give her a certain version of the truth that made, at least, articulate sense and didn't sound too stupid. Now she has Nigel Lawson and Mr John Redwood of the Centre for Policy Studies, sitting in his Think Tank (which is not, I'm assured, rhyming slang after all).

MONEY SUPPLY
DEFINITION #425
"STINKY AND
MUCKY"

And what do they do, these babes in the wood? Poor Nigel keeps changing his measure of money supply in a desperate attempt to set a target they might, just, possibly, meet, and the others bleat about 'tax cuts' (a fine piece of Thatcherite rhetoric that soon takes on the appearance of a security blanket to nuzzle up to in moments of crisis) that haven't happened yet (rather the opposite, in fact), and neither are they likely to. Meantime, Nigel searches high and low for a structure that makes it all make sense. Sterling M3? Nope, done that; didn't work. PSL2? What dat? Well, it's Private Sector Liquidity 2, er, y'know, Sterling M3 plus a bit . . . Ur, what about M0? Well, it must mean something, mustn't it? ML&D? What's that? Um, it's Money Supply Loopy and Dappy, all the money in the piggy banks and what loose change I can find in my turn-ups. What? Look, I've got a tummy-ache, can't all you people leave me alone?

So much for attempts to run the economy. But here, of course, comes the great contradiction. If Thatcherism were truly, fundamentally monetarist, a genuine exercise in nostalgia in returning to Victorian *laissez-faire*, if it really wanted to get 'government off the backs of the people' and it actually listened to its intellectual *manqué* mentors, then, on her first being elected, Thatcher would have immediately resigned and set about dismantling the machinery of central government. You wanna free market? Then here it is, suckers! But life isn't like that, is it? And what the Government giveth, so too the Government taketh away . . .

In the light of this, we might consider two curious developments. You will recall what I said earlier about this obsession with economics taking on an almost Marxist flavour. This is not, I think, a freak. Indeed, in many ways the Thatcher Governments have proved to be exactly like the nightmare far-left Governments foreseen in the constitutional text books: the erosion of civil liberties with increased powers for the police and the organs of state security and surveillance; the politicization of the judiciary and the civil service; the use of the short enabling bill to suspend elections and abolish the Metropolitan County Councils and the GLC. Even the media is seen as an enemy, and we have the marvellous sight of Tory Tony Benns, twitching with paranoia under the studio lights and accusing the BBC of gross political bias as they try to explain how the Conservative candidate losing his deposit is, in fact, a major victory for the Government and an unparalleled disaster for the other five parties.

What? Did all those musty old constitutionalists see the revolution coming from the wrong direction? Somehow, I feel we cannot entirely account the Thatcherites as revolutionaries: there is posturing, but no programme, and policy seems to be dreamt up on impulse and from pique. Thus the abolition of the GLC, inspired by a dislike of Ken Livingstone and duly written, at the last moment, into the '83 Manifesto. (Speaking of manifestoes, we might do well to remember Lord Denning's Fares Fair judgement, when he said that manifesto promises didn't count for anything; this should have been pointed out to Patrick Jenkin, if anyone thought he had an attention span long enough to accommodate it.)

And this impulsiveness leads us to the other development.

Tipped out of her *seda gestatoria* and deserted by her tame academics,

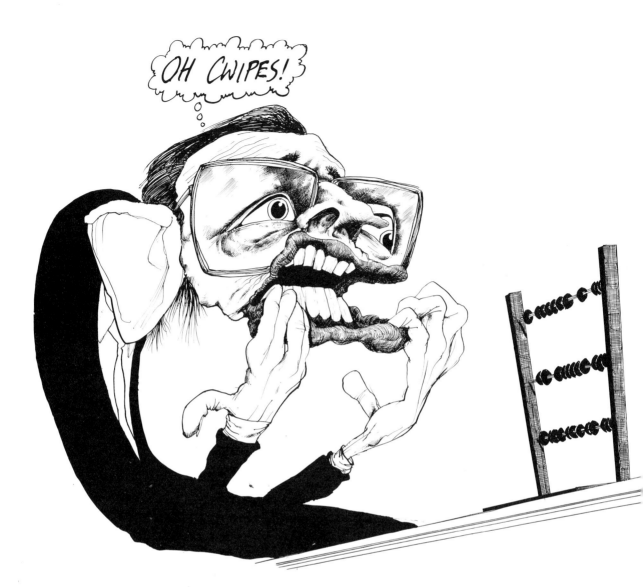

Thatcher's gone rogue. Although it now seems she and her supporters are in a minority in the Cabinet, there remains the urge to introduce policies, not because they make any sense, but because they might bolster up the image. Like Nixon in his second term, surrounded by unseen enemies and raving that 'when the going gets tough, the tough get going', Thatcher is now seeing what she can get away with in order to show how 'tough' and 'resolute' she is. To take just one instance, look at the proposed abolition of State Earnings Related Pensions. You can imagine the excitement they must have felt at this great 'reform' of the Welfare State, whooping and howling in the Cabinet room as Norman Fowler grinned crazily over his epidiascope. Why, they even made a promise, just before the last election, in writing, that they weren't going to do away with this one, but the hell with that. Their eyes glazed over as they thought on their daring and took up the chorus 'We've really got 'em this time' until it echoed round the room, engulfing the stern figure of the Prime Minister at the head of the table, standing in her Churchill pose. But then, oh dear, all alone afterwards Norman began to have doubts. Could they really get away with this? And the more he brooded, the more he worried, until, late into the night, he belted round to the printers where, even as he arrived, the Green Paper was on the presses. Too late! But maybe not, and pushing aside the complaining typesetters, he pulled out all those incriminating figures, tears of relief clouding his vision. No figures? No problem! The amazed printers stood back in wonder and reached for the blunt instruments . . .

As I've said before, in incautious moments one can almost begin to feel sorry for these people, muddling through as best they can, spouting empty rhetoric, trying to come on tough and then thinking up an approximation of a policy to back up the wild words. But we haven't yet touched on Thatcher's greatest piece of rhetoric, all this nonsense about Victorian values, in which quarter at least she's making some headway.

Having no sense of history, Thatcher doesn't exactly know what she means when she talks about Victorian values, but it sounds pretty neat if you don't think about it too much. If you do think about it, however, your position as Prime Minister becomes a little uneasy. A *grocer's* DAUGHTER? Not the kind of thing that would have gone down too well during Lord Aberdeen's Ministry, I should have thought. But, that aside, the achievements are many, in some ways going beyond the original. Indeed, the regulations on the unemployed staying in guest houses are well on the way to creating an itinerant population of sturdy beggars to rival that of the first Elizabethans. Meanwhile, the ill-conceived and petulant plans for the Metropolitan Counties should, when implemented, re-create an almost Dickensian state of affairs, and, moreover, current plans to abolish the Public Health Laboratory Service should ensure that the inner-city slums are once more, as in Great Victoria's glorious reign, the court of King Cholera. And with interest rates the same in real terms at the moment as they were during the Napoleonic Wars, we begin to see what a truly remarkable programme of policies this is; if effected, what a magnificent achievement, what a lasting monument to one woman's dream!

But still, as always, there are problems. Problems, and two years into her second term, with everything falling to bits about her, no one to trust and her enemies closing in all the time, Mrs Thatcher still feels the need, yearns for the counsel, nay more, the comforting presence of her familiar, her dear, dear Cecil. He, at least, understood her vision; acted on it; embodied it. Oh yes, Cecil certainly showed the way with his celebration of that greatest of all Victorian values: hypocrisy . . .

OPPOSITION? WHAT OPPOSITION?

Away from Thatcher's stabs at an economic policy where, like Alice in *Through the Looking Glass*, you have to run just as fast as you can simply to stay in one place, to another nonsense world.

As on previous occasions on this trip of mine, the place I now find myself was not my chosen destination. I caught the wrong train. But, then again, there is

much to be said for serendipity. When I turned up in Pyongyang, for instance, who could have foreseen that I would spend a pleasant evening with poor old Prince Sianouk, a man I'd previously avoided like the plague and for whom I still have mixed feelings? Why, I even bought him dinner, and in return he told me a rather funny story about Henry Kissinger. Still, here I am in Milton Keynes, and I wonder whether to go exploring or wait for the first train out.

What, for instance, does the place have to offer? From the TV adverts one sees, it seems to have only one industry: promoting itself. In 500 years' time, when the regimented rows of ticky-tacky houses have taken on a certain period charm, will there still be adverts imploring people to come to picturesque old Milton Keynes to witness the rich and ancient pageantry of the balloon ceremony, its origins lost in a mythic past? Or view the concrete cows, marking the centuries with immobile witness like the petrified lovers of Pompeii? And will the citizens of the future wonder at the barbarity performed each day at dawn as the world's last angler, under strict licence, cycles slowly through the tourists to his bloodthirsty hobby? Questions, questions, none of which I'm inclined to illustrate by direct experience, so I'll stick it here and continue wondering.

Ah me, Milton Keynes: sport for all and a Volvo in every driveway; a barracks for Thatcher's army. As I've already observed, the most important consideration about Thatcher's vision for Britain is that it is *boring*, and here in Milton Keynes we have a taste of that future. There is something indefinably disagreeable about sunlight on concrete and tarmac, about brave new squash courts filled with healthy, smiling, fit young executives keeping in trim while their wives keep the home central heating burning and inflate countless balloons for their grinning offspring. It's a ghastly combination of strength-through-joy Outward Boundism (I belong to a school which regards all sudden movements as ill-bred), a belief in the higher truths of advertising copy and fresh-faced middle class endeavour: in short, what Thatcherism is all about when you unclutter it of the music hall jingo and the Gradgrindism of the Victorian values rhetoric. Muesli in every bowl! Highland Spring Water in every champagne flute given away with every £10 worth of petrol for the wife's runabout. Yikes! The apotheosis of Suburbia with, in the rural idylls of Milton Keynes, a few corn dollies displayed in the steel and concrete sports hall for good measure . . .

Here we have the people who've done well out of Thatcherism, who like the middle class in the first seven or eight years of Pinochet's Chile, view the full shops and prefer not to consider the shanty towns where the bulk of the population starves and lies victim to the Secret Police: the torturable class.

But, then again, here in Milton Keynes we also have the headquarters of the SDP.

And yet, is it unreasonable to say that the SDP is a distinctly Thatcherite phenomenon? Certainly, on the simplest level, it would have been impossible without Thatcherism, without the polarization to left and right of the two major parties, leaving room in the middle ground for two others. But beyond that, I think we can say there is a marked similarity between whatever philosophy it is that guides the SDP and the philosophy of Thatcherism, with only surface differences: thus, where Thatcherism wishes to create its New Jerusalem according to the principles of the Ideal Home Exhibition, the SDP would look to the credos of the time-share holiday seminar; where Thatcherism's hymns are sung in the rhetoric of the tupperware party, the SDP's are couched in the argot of the smarter wine and cheese party. In short, the SDP is Thatcherism with a human face; or, more correctly, with less of a lower-middle, suburban, and more of a middle-middle, urban face.

To clarify this, we might digress for a moment and consider the *Zeitgeister* distinct to the different parties: thus it's forward into the 1870s with the Tories, into the 1930s with Labour, and onward into the 1960s with the SDP. Ah yes, the Sixties: the Great Society vision of shopping malls and ring roads that's become flesh, for the lucky ones, in the Eighties, with the fantastic realization that you can buy cheap wine in a plastic bag and get rich without necessarily feeling guilty about it. And, in qualifying your attitude to this state of mind, you choose your party. If you go on not feeling guilty about anything, and enjoy being bombastic, odious and rude to social workers at parties, then you vote Conservative; if, on the other hand, you like feeling a bit guilty about one or two things of not much significance the better to feed your smugness, but still can't bring yourself to make public your real feelings about social workers, then you vote SDP. In other words, the SDP is all about not having the bottle to go the whole hog and do a Reg Prentice.

Ah yes, but what about the alliance with the Liberals?

Dr. David Owen moves strangely RIGHTWARDS...

I remember at the time of the Limehouse Declaration that a good number of naïve people asked why the Gang of Four were messing around with this strange construction 'The Council for Social Democracy'; why, in short, they didn't just go straight away and join the Liberals. Such speculations fail to understand the mentality behind the SDP, however, and therefore fail to understand the fundamental differences between it and the Liberal Party. For while the latter is an ancient party which has learnt to bide its time and divert its energies to petitioning for cycle tracks on the trunk roads and the preservation of badgers – in short, to be generally *nice* – the Social Democrats, coming from a different tradition, are impatient for power. Bearing in mind Harold Wilson's celebrated adage 'a week is a long time in politics', one gets the impression that the Social Democrats are quite unable to remember the beginning of the week by the time it's Wednesday, and thereafter are incapable of waiting for the weekend. Thus, when it looked as if the Right's dominance of the Labour Party was waning, rather than biding their time as the Left had done for the previous twenty years, the Social Democrats-to-be immediately upped and formed a party of their own that they could dominate to their hearts' content.

Of course, all this was surrounded by a great deal of humbug about 'unacceptable changes in the great Party I have loved and served for forty years' and so on, but at its centre the SDP is obsessed with the dream for power. Thus, at its instigation the SDP had but four firm policies: that Roy Jenkins should be Prime Minister; that Shirley Williams should be Prime Minister; that David Owen should be Prime Minister; and, when they'd all had a bash at it, that William Rodgers could be Prime Minister, too. (Now, of course, they only have one policy.) And otherwise it is left a matter for conjecture what else the SDP stands for (Smugness Denotes Power? Simply Delightful Poses?), believes in, proposes (on the long, empty days succeeding that happy dawn) *to do*.

I should imagine all this must put an almost intolerable strain on the Alliance. That surfeit of Great Statesmen – Roy Jenkins, of whom it was tellingly said 'the only thing he's ever fought for is a table for two at Maxim's'; Shirley Williams, summed up by Denis Healey with the words 'just because she never combs her hair and wears big chunky sweaters she thinks she's a socialist'; Dr Death himself, the greatest Foreign Secretary since Palmerston, the tactician of genius behind the Falklands victory, the cunning Kingmaker who holds the balance of power in his old sawbones' hands – and the way the poor, naïve Liberals must be intimidated by men like Ian Wrigglesworth (ah yes, and what a man – who can think up really neat plans for the Economy off the top of his head, confident in the knowledge that he'll never have to put them into practice). And the problems go further. Not only do the Liberals keep thinking up sensible policies at their Conferences that go against all that the SDP holds dear – as when the Conference voted for the removal of Cruise (and outside, on the seafront, Bill Rodgers brushed the hair from his eyes and boldly announced, 'Well, this is why the Liberals are much better than the Labour Party. This decision counts for nothing with the leadership') – but there's also the problem of the difference in style. Thus the sad predicament of those Tammany Hall Labour politicians who got out just before they were found out, relieved that they'd no longer have to bluster to the CLP and try to park their Mercs between the bikes of the feared and hated 'activists', only to find that outside the Liberal Club the car park's just as full of bicycles as ever it was outside the Co-op. Then, when the poor old buffer gets inside and hangs up his cavalry coat, there's the hall filled with aggressive activists and bearded men in dungarees all over again.

But what of the future? With the Liberals as soft-option Labour, and the SDP as soft-option Conservative, if the Alliance holds the balance of power after the next election there are going to be even more problems when the groups start shifting around trying to make pacts. It's obvious that the Labour Party won't do a deal with Owen, the Great Quitter, and, likewise, he is unlikely to forgive them for not allowing him to become their leader five years ago; but then I should also say that the Liberals are disinclined to come to an accommodation with Thatcher. The Alliance will, therefore, split, and if it looks likely that this will result in the formation of a Government, the Liberals will enter into a pact with Labour. The SDP, meanwhile, will count its losses, kick its heels for a while and finally fall in with the Tories. And, having no history – moreover, no sense of history and no traditions beyond some half-baked memories of Hugh Gaitskell – it will disappear in a post-Thatcher Conservative party, making room for Sir Terence Beckett's prophecy to come true: that, after Thatcher, the Tories will be led by either Norman Tebbit or David Owen, and David Owen can become Prime Minister after all, and his supporters can, at long last, stop feeling guilty about anything and open another bag of Beaujolais.

(I should now point out, however, that I've always considered fortune-telling a futile activity, and anyway the next Leader of the Conservative Party is going to be Geoffrey Howe.)

Still, it should be said in the SDP's favour that it, at least, recognized, however unwittingly, that Thatcherism represented a change in the rules; here was something quite new that required a new antithesis, a new synthesis. So, if you can't beat 'em . . . Thus an interesting new approach to opposition, where it's assumed that, if you want the votes, you ought to do what the people who are getting the votes at the moment are doing, and those people foolish enough to believe Thatcher's rhetoric about there being no alternative begin to see, in Dr Owen, an alternative they can fully accommodate without compromising their beliefs.

For those involved in genuine opposition, it took rather longer to wake up to the new reality. Thus, for the first five years of Thatcherism triumphant, the Labour Party and the Trade Unions carried on playing the old game. (It is true that in a decent society a sweet old man like Michael Foot would be elected President for Life and comfort the people with nightly readings from Hazlitt, but, as I've said before, Thatcher's about the business of creating a society with no room for gentlemen, where 'decency' is what Norman Fowler comes out with when he's trying to say 'defence strategy'.) Likewise, the Trade Union barons don't achieve much either for themselves or for their members when their only consideration is how to get back into No. 10 for beer and sandwiches, just like in the old days with Jim – even if, when they get there, wrapped up in their 'new

realism', the Prime Minister makes them stand while she sips champagne, doesn't even offer them a biscuit, and ends the meeting marching up and down in her stiletto heels on the prostrate form of poor Len Murray.

What these people failed to grasp, I think, was that, when the rules have changed once, you can carry on changing them, make them up just as fast as you can and keep the other bloke on the hop. Failure to appreciate this has resulted in a thousand and one missed opportunities for hitting Thatcherism where it hurts the most, by making it look ridiculous. A couple of instances, then, of what might have been.

When the Pentagon told Thatcher to impose a union ban at GCHQ (to sustain the non-secret of America's exact role in the Falklands War: see the entry under 12th June), instead of talking bravely about natural justice and standing hard on high principle, the union should have said, okay then, we accept in theory the idea that civil liberties can be bought and sold, but come off it! £1000? This is a joke! Worse, an insult! £25,000 minimum, each, is what we're talking about here, and you can take it or leave it. The Government, able to understand thinking like this, would certainly have taken it, and thus been seen as willing to squander vast amounts of public money in pursuit of a feeble principle. Likewise, when legislation was introduced to oblige the unions to vote on their political levies in a crude attempt to pauperize the Labour Party, the National Executive of that party should have announced, just for a giggle, that this was fine, and that it would be written into the next manifesto that every company that subscribes to Tory Party funds would be nationalized within half an hour of a Labour victory, the better to protect their shareholders' interests.

You would think that making Thatcher and the Thatcherites look ridiculous would be a relatively simple task, and yet, unfortunately for the general entertainment of the people, the Labour Party has chosen the serious option, coming across as hard-nosed professionals itching to get down to the job in hand. That they've done this by choosing, within the context of the Labour Party, the demagogic path, and meeting Thatcherism half-way there by hiring the PR men and the advertising agents, is a shame, but seems typical of the Kinnock approach; and, as he does his merry dance to distance himself from anything that might contaminate the image that he's anywhere to the left of Sir Ian Gilmour or any more threatening than Stanley Baldwin, we'll just have to see where it gets him.

Opposition? What opposition?

Certainly in Parliament (and as almost any political action outside Parliament is seen as little short of Red revolution and regicide) the business of opposition seems a futile one. Inasmuch as Thatcher clearly wants to outdo Mr Gladstone and rule into her nineties, one can't quite make the comparison with the deranged President in his second term, free to do as he would without fear of electoral retribution ('Hey, Bob, will ya quit editing them tapes a minute? I'm bored. Howza bout we drop the bomb? Exterminate them all?'), but none the less, with her massive parliamentary majority Thatcher can get away with almost anything, confident in the knowledge that, should she finally make up her mind and go for it, kicking out the jams by abolishing the House of Lords and

disestablishing the Church of England, the suburban daleks of the 1922 Committee will still trundle faithfully through the lobbies, blindly obedient to the last.

Could it be, then, that there really is no alternative? That, as Adlai Stevenson observed, a country gets the Government it deserves? That Britain has finally sunk so low that there is now a permanent majority of somnambulists, lulled into cosy comas by the wombnal hum of magimixers and videos whirring away in their own council houses or suburban villas, modernized with a second mortgage and, dependent on the degree of their indifference or nastiness, either going the whole hog with Mrs Thatcher or else salving their conscience with a vote for Trojan Owen and, as happened in 1983, splitting the opposition to allow the Tories to sneak back in and to ensure Thatcher her majority in perpetuity?

You never can tell. After all, I've had a glimpse of the future. I've seen the concrete cows lowing through the Astroturf as ever more balloons are inflated and, protected by a moat of ring roads from the surrounding wreckage, the happy castellans pull another stopper from yet another bag of bitter wine.

FINAL ENCOUNTERS WITH AGREEABLE FRIENDS

LONDON ZOO,
15 OCTOBER 1985

'Animals are such agreeable friends – they ask no questions, they pass no criticisms' GEORGE ELIOT

Holland Park is once more mine. Much has happened since July, but all is forgotten when a 'phone call from Heathrow gets me the answering machine again, and a brief message granting me ingress to the family pile. However, when I arrive, not only are Helen and the children not there, but neither is any of the furniture. A message, written on the wall in lipstick, reads: 'Gone with Jacques. See you around. Helen.' Jacques? Can't be Lacan again, as he's dead. Derrida? I despair, briefly, at my ex-wife's persistent fondness for French mountebanks, and consider what all this implies about Thatcher's philosophy of home comforts and family life, now revealed like so much else as fantastic and offensive bullshit.

Ah well, there you go, but instead of brooding on such things I've taken advantage of the Luke's Day Summer to return to the Zoo, a still centre of peace and calm in an otherwise chaotic world. And yet, even here, the palsied hand of Thatcherism intrudes: there have been attempts to raise money by turning the place into a fun fair; and can it be too long before life begins to reflect art and, as in *The Old Men at the Zoo*, social malcontents are fed to the animals to pull in the fee-paying public and the poor brutes are presented in tableaux of the market forces at work?

Worse yet, I find my former pupil gazing uneasily into the cage housing Humboldt's gibbon. However, two months in the deserts have clearly mellowed me and this time I do not flee; somehow I feel that I have nothing to fear, here on home ground, so I tap the little chap on the shoulder and he turns round with a start.

'What does it mean?' he asks, chewing his lower lip, his eyes darting around wildly. 'I mean, why? What is the purpose of this animal? What does it do? Can you buy it? Sell it? I just don't understand.' And, as so often before on this odyssey, I feel an uncontrollable pity for the callous little punk, his lower lip trembling as he tries to make sense of and engage in inter-species contact with a contented beast who has nothing but contempt for him. Housed, fed, free to do as it will and freed from the tyranny of the jungle, the gibbon stands – rather, sits, hunched up and scratching itself – as a glowing tribute to Welfareism. You could say, of course, that the gibbon cannot possibly be content without his freedom, but then again, what would he do if the cage door was opened? Dodge the traffic on the Euston Road and pick through the bins in search for food, be cruelly spurned by the DHSS because of his non-human status and then get soundly whacked by the police, confused into fury by his fur and refusal to answer their questions? These are the opportunities for freedom as peddled by dubious advocates like my former pupil here, deep in the heart of Thatcher's Britain.

Still, seeing the little freedom fighter in such low spirits, I offer him a drink in the Members' Bar, where he sneers at the decor, is rude to the barman and drinks a great deal of crème de menthe. Attempting conversation, I ask him what he thinks of the Government's present fortunes, about the new riots,

Jeffrey Archer, the Cabinet reshuffle, the zany idea that
'presentation' is at the root of all his Party's ills. His
answers astound, but do not surprise me. Archer . . . great
communicator . . . common touch . . . new blood . . .
message must get across . . . Kremlin and Tripoli
agitators. And then the litany of the New Right starts
all over again. Missed opportunities . . . still a
chance at making the dream work . . . Wealth
Creation . . . Enterprise Culture . . . Great Challenges
. . . I try to ask him about Cecil Parkinson, and then
to cheer him up by telling him that today's
Nietzsche's 141st birthday, but he doesn't hear me
so I switch off.

And, in the same way that my mind wandered
laterally at the beginning of these reflections all
those months ago, my thoughts now turn, for no
particular reason, to Stalin, and a final image of
Thatcher occurs, one her packagers would never
think of in a thousand years.

Thatcher as Stalin? Surely not. And yet the more I think about it, the more it attracts me. Sitting out in her Dulwich dacha going slowly mad, quite convinced that she is surrounded by enemies, able to trust no one and consumed with a philosophy of hatred, while still trying to find time to pose beside the crumbling hydro-electric dams and kid the world she has messianic powers when she places her hands on the bedridden who can't escape: Great Mother of the People.

There are further parallels. The phoney toughness to disguise general funk; the encouraged paranoia about 'alien influence' and conniving foreigners; the attitude to underlings and all this nonsense about 'presentation'.

It has been widely observed that the problem of presentation is due not to the failure of 'getting the message across' but, conversely, its success, and the Government's been rumbled. But of course we can hardly expect Thatcher to see that, in order to make the Conservative Party attractive to the electorate again, she ought to do the decent thing and resign immediately, taking all her creatures with her as she returns to that low stratum of social existence from which she was cruelly dragged by the queenmakers. No, no, it's all about presentation, and thus the Cabinet reshuffle, Norman Tebbit and Jeffrey Archer.

All of which reminds me of one of Stalin's few essays in internal public relations, when the NKVD under Yagoda was causing considerable unease among the Soviet people with its policy of terror. In order to put their minds at rest, Stalin simply abolished the NKVD, arrested Yagoda and all his operatives, shot them and replaced them with the OGPU under N. I. Yezhov. Which trick worked for about six months, until the people realized that things were now, if anything, worse than before, and the terror escalated.

Norman Tebbit the Yezhov to Gummer's Yagoda? But let us remain for a while longer in the madhouse of Stalin's Russia during the era of the Show Trials, when Ministers unlucky enough to draw the short straw as this week's scapegoat admitted to fantastic and horrendous crimes 'for the good of the Party': just as Mrs Thatcher's loyal stooges, having done her dirty work for her, have publicly been happy to resign for the 'good of the Party'. And, as many people wonder what exactly was going on in the minds of men like Zinoviev and Kamenev as they blandly announced their plot to murder Stalin hatched in a non-existent hotel in Stockholm with Trotsky (who was in France at the time), we must ask: did poor Patrick Jenkin know what he did? Did he do enough, or should he have made the ultimate sacrifice for the good of the Party and walked into County Hall with the bomb strapped beneath his raincoat? Still, there are plenty more where he came from, and where Leon Brittan came from, too, and all willing to implement policies they don't believe in but are too fearful to question.

But we should be wary of taking the metaphor too far. After all, all attempts to build up a cult of the personality around Mrs Thatcher seem to have failed, and the worst she can really do to her Ministers is sack them or send them off to Ulster, her equivalent of the Power Station in Ulan Bator. Moreover, it would be quite preposterous to compare Norman Tebbit to Laventry Beria, ignorant in the use of knife and fork and smiling sweetly as he impressed upon the party faithful the necessity of being cruel to be kind; or to see anything familiar in the Government's efforts to criminalize political dissent, or to account the urban riots to the work of 'criminal elements' and 'outside agitators'; or to wonder at all about the increasing politicization of the police force; or to observe how Thatcherism has succeeded in creating millions and millions of internal exiles from her exclusive dream of the Crusade towards a Better Capitalism, the Free Market Police State where the loyal cadres shout 'Slavery is Freedom!'

But it's not like that at all, is it? And Jeffrey Archer leans forward and glowers with a look like thunder; Stalin was a Communist, wasn't he? Everyone knows that. I mean, he was Russian for a start. And Mrs Thatcher certainly isn't a Communist. Oh no, she's a Capitalist, and a damn good thing it is, too. The Deputy Chairman pauses to allow the puckish daring of his foul mouth to sink in, and to try to remember what the back room boys told him earlier on. 'She's the Chairman of Great Britain Limited, and you and I are both shareholders!' And with that the Disraeli of today's Tory Party leans back with a smirk and a friendly snarl.

Ah yes, and there you have it. Great Britain, Limited, and we're all in the business of making money. Indeed, as Jeffrey observed during an unhappy radio

NOW LISTEN HERE, YOU B.B.C. **ROTTER**, IF YOU CAN SPEAK ANYTHING OTHER THAN **LIBYAN**, THAT IS! WHEN I SAID THE UNEMPLOYED WERE A BUNCH OF **BONE-IDLE BOLSHEVIK BASTARDS** & **THAT** THE CONSERVATIVE PARTY COULDN'T DAM' WELL RUN A PISS-UP IN A **DISTILLARY**, I DIDN'T SAY ANYTHING OF THE SORT, GOT ME?

interview, 'When I pay £45,000 in income tax *a year*, I think I have a *right* to *serve!*' Well, yes, and a plutocracy is just fine, and a competently run one even better. And yet Archer is hardly in a position, as a former bankrupt, to bully the rest of us about the sweet thrill of enterprise, no more than Douglas Hurd ('So you've lived in Handsworth all your life? And this is your garden? Jolly good! And these are your . . .' THWACK!!!) does much for the disenfranchised black Britons of the abandoned inner cities by telling them they are aliens and criminals, nor does Norman Tebbit reassure us greatly that Conservatives care when he looks as if he's just bitten the head off a weasel. Nor do any of them instil faith

IT'S ALRIGHT, I'VE BEEN TO BELFAST... IT'S ALRIGHT, I'VE BEEN TO BELFAST... IT'S ALRIGHT...

BONK!

by howling and pawing the ground and barking off the same stale clichés, half-remembered from the shamans of the Chicago School, while the Government officiates over the dismantling of the Welfare State, the harrying of free education, the destruction of civil liberties and the worst instances of civil unrest for forty years, and leaves the country Thatcher and her party profess to love and cherish above all else in chaos and collapse.

But is the social Luddism of the Thatcherites mischievous, or simply the product of cold-blooded incompetence? I believe the mischief was probably there at the beginning, dressed up as cod policy, but a lot of the wreckage is the result of an inability to admit that the whole thing has gone hopelessly wrong, and, believing there to be simple answers and simple explanations and simple cures, Thatcherism, with its cultivation of the brutal and banal, hunkers down in the dug-out, sulkily growling, 'We'll show 'em, ungrateful bastards. Think they know better, eh? Just you wait and see. Yeah, we'll show 'em and they'll be *really* sorry this time . . .'

But is this really the end for the shop counter-revolution? After all, she's been here before, the most unpopular Prime Minister in history, her policies in ruins, the streets in tumult, and it could just be she'll go for broke, seeing there's nothing to lose, and plan another reshuffle, her opportunity arising when

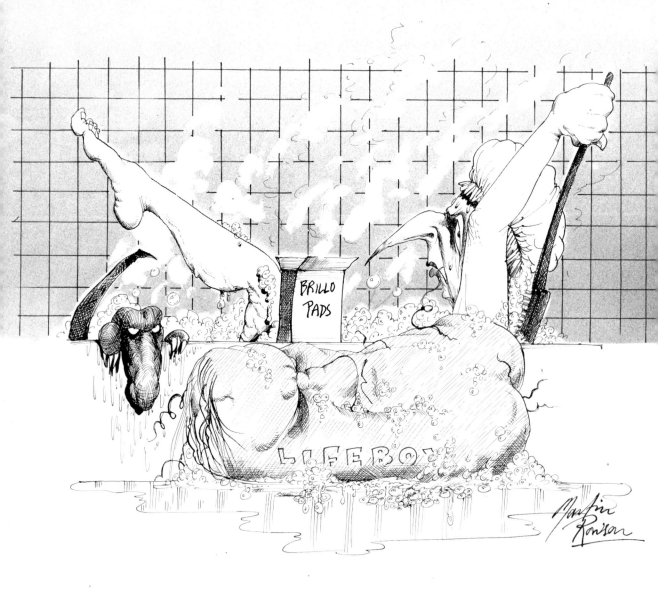

Archer's caught on 'Breakfast Time' kicking an argumentative dancing parrot to within an inch of its life, and she can get Cecil back . . . (And another brief digression on Cecil Parkinson: someone told me the other day that Parkinson reminded them of nothing so much as a bar of soap, white and translucent sitting on the edge of the bath, with a layer of gelatinous slime underneath, and strangely sensuous and disgusting when it slips between the cleft of your buttocks.)

Imagine the scene, a year or so hence, the first Cabinet after the reshuffle finished, the cowed Ministers sloping off to a low bar for a well-needed drink, and Thatcher and Parkinson alone together at last.

'Well,' breathes the Prime Minister huskily, the past all forgotten as she stares indulgently at the returned prodigal, 'what do you think we should do?'

'Well,' says the Great Communicator, 'um, ah, well, we, ah . . .'

And then the news comes in that the cod-hungry Icelanders have invaded Rockall, and here we go again.

Would the country fall for it again? Is Britain really now like the potential suicide who, having swallowed the bottle of pills, then reaches for the whisky jar?

Perhaps I'm getting a bit mawkish, but I've just found my old friend the orang-utan again, now moved from the Great Apes Breeding House and sitting in the midst of his enlarged family, picking his nose and sticking damp bits of straw into his children's ears. He refuses to recognize me, but clearly, when the trippers went home, they finally got it together and, in a moment of simian bliss, did it. Life, in spite of all, goes on, and I retract the libel with which I commenced these thoughts on Thatcherism. No, the anthropomorphic thesis doesn't work, for Thatcher stocks her plastic jungle with wholly different, wilder and weirder animals in her bid to build a better Britain out of Velcro, Vaseline and plutonium. For myself, I now choose to put aside all further thoughts of Thatcher in all or any of her manifestations, and her philosophy, her acolytes, and the nightmare of a plastic world buzzing with cash registers and peopled by callous, artless and uncomplaining homunculi that she tries to peddle as her dream of Cockeyne. Instead, I'm off to rejoin my furry, feathered and scaly chums back in the Zoo.

APPENDIX

Martin Rowson writes: The following is a letter. I received from Killane outlining his first thoughts on the Westland Helicopter affair, which reached a head in January 1986 with the resignation of the Defence Secretary, Michael Heseltine, one of Killane's chief *bêtes noires*.

> VILLA DIAGHILEV,
> BIARRITZ, MIDNIGHT,
> 14 JANUARY 1986

Dear Rowson

Well, the shit has really hit the fan this time, and I am set thinking by the reports coming in over the World Service about the Westland business, the Heseltine resignation and much else. Is this really the end for Thatcherism? Will Heseltine really bring her down in his sudden conversion to the principles of freedom of information? Can this be Profumo rewritten to suit a less exalted age? Is he getting his revenge on Thatcher for making him Secretary of State for Defence in the first place, a job in which he was neither especially successful, nor beloved of his civil servants? Or, best joke of all, is he cutting and running, leaving some other poor placeman to clear up the wreckage? Or was it simply just another Central Office ruse to divert attention from the unemployment figures published the same day as this resignation farrago?

Personally, all I can think about is how that vainglorious thug has, in a typically ill-conceived and revoltingly boisterous public relations exercise, in his bid to become Prime Minister, cancelled out all I said about him last summer. Can you salvage something from this?

Also, has Helen been in touch? Oh, God damn and blast them all to hell.

Yours,

Kevin Killane, Ph. D.